The Great Outdoors
Book of the Walking Year

The Great Outdoors Book of the Walking Year

Edited by ROGER SMITH

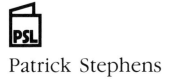

Patrick Stephens

Front endpaper *Peter Dale, Derbyshire in early spring* (Richard Gilbert).

Rear endpaper *Winter dawn over the Home Counties, Olney, Buckinghamshire* (G.J. Truscott).

British Library Cataloguing in Publication Data

The Great Outdoors book of the walking year.
  1. Walking
I. Smith, Roger, 1938–
796.5'1'0922   GV199.5

ISBN 0-85059-935-0

Patrick Stephens Limited is part of the Thorsons Publishing Group, Wellingborough, Northamptonshire, NN8 2RQ, England.

Printed in Great Britain by Butler & Tanner Limited, Frome, Somerset.

10 9 8 7 6 5 4 3 2 1

Contents

Introduction

Anyone who walks regularly for recreation becomes sharply aware of the changing seasons, of the time of year, of the weather and the state of the day — in fact of the whole temporal environment around him (or her). My own experiences in all twelve months of the year and in as many countries have led me to a greatly heightened sense of the cycle of the year, so that 'earth' dates such as equinoxes and solstices assume a very real significance.

That feeling is the inspiration for this book and I hope that after reading it you will feel, as I do, that it was a happy inspiration indeed. We have set our eleven contributors the task of summarizing their feelings about a particular month and right well they have done it. From Peter Wilson's sharp January inscription of the Lake District through to Colin Speakman's affectionate portrait of the Dales in December, every month comes through with its own identity and its own feeling for the walker.

In nature of course, the year is almost seamless, but Man must always be dividing and measuring, cutting things into segments that he can grasp. These are not, however, twelve separate segments, distinct in character though they are, but a shifting kaleidoscope of impressions moving through the year in an order which is somehow nevertheless highly satisfying.

One of the delights for me in my time as editor of *Great Outdoors* has been to find so many enthusiastic writers who were competent photographers (or better) as well, and in this book all twelve chapters are illustrated by the authors' own efforts with a camera. I thank the publishers for hiding my own modest efforts at capturing July on film so well amongst such splendour!

We set out to make a book that would be enjoyable to read and which had an identifiable theme that readers who are themselves walkers would easily relate to. In that I hope we have succeeded. Certainly for my part it has been a great joy to put together and I thank the eleven good friends and colleagues whose efforts go to make it up. My own chapter I leave for you, the reader, to judge.

Whatever your 'favourite' time of year, if you have such a thing, you will find it here — no-one can say their 'best' month for walking is omitted! The places visited range from the far north of Scotland to the eastern United States, but much of the book is concerned with the land we British know best, and the countryside which is still a source of such immense pleasure to so many people from all over the world. Unlike many books, there is no particular need to start this one at the beginning. Dip into it where you will, according to whichever month you feel suits your mood. We start the book with the calendar, in January, but if you'd rather read about June in the Pyrenees first, please open these pages as you like.

My thanks to all who have helped in the preparation of the book, in particular my editor, Graham Truscott, for his patience and understanding. I hope that all concerned and you, the reader, are as happy with the result as I am.

Roger Smith, November 1987

The summer view into upper Eskdale from Harter Fell, with the Scafell range beyond (Geoffrey N. Wright).

January in the Lakeland Fells

PETER WILSON

For me January, and in particular the New Year holiday, has come to be synonymous with the Lake District and is as good an excuse as any other to escape to the hills. I have combined New Year celebrations with several days' fell-walking for more years than I care to remember but I still do not tire of tramping those glorious hills, neatly tucked away into the finest corner of England. As winter approaches and weather forecasts report 'snow on high ground', the anticipation and excitement grow apace. Snow covered peaks, frozen becks and tarns and bright cloudless skies are the conditions that give the fells their winter appeal and charm, but January is an unpredictable month — a month when sharp meteorological contrasts can be expected.

Snow and frost occur frequently but almost equally likely are still, sunlit days lacking snow, or wild, wet days with driving rain sweeping across the hills and visibility reduced to a matter of yards. Days of cold rain and gales are common enough at this time of year, as befits the British winter, but there is often that element of surprise in the weather too. Several days of shocking conditions may suddenly give way to a calm, sunny morning with the snow-plastered fells rising gracefully towards the deep blue of the skies. When this happens, the mantle of snow and ice lends to the hills an air of mystery. Modest Lakeland fells usually seem bigger and more remote — with a grandeur akin to Alpine peaks. To tread the high snows on such occasions and see the sharp, distant horizons is ample compensation for the numerous wind-blasted and rain-lashed days endured, and brings the height of exhilaration to the keen winter fell walker.

January is also a quiet month in Lakeland. Gone are the summer hordes and the associated clamour. The towns and villages are transformed, almost unrecognizable, and life is taken at a more sedate pace. The hills and dales are in the midst of a long, deep sleep and there is little to disturb the tranquility that descends over the fell-country. For these reasons, winter fell-walking is an understandably popular activity amongst the keener breed of hikers. Ask any experienced walker to recall his most memorable day in the hills and he will probably describe a winter walk over the high tops with a dazzling sun and brilliant blue sky above, firm virgin snow underfoot and the hills peaceful and empty.

My January visits to Lakeland extend to many different valleys but New Year is invariably spent in Borrowdale and these days have provided some of my most treasured mountain experiences. The hills are rewarding in all months and seasons of the year, yet if I was allowed only one more visit to Lakeland I would unhesitatingly choose January and hope for one or two of those magical sun-kissed days that have caused me to return time and again. Let me try to describe some of them.

New Year's Day always sees some fells climbed if at all possible. The weather normally dictates how far and high we go, but the festivities of the previous evening can take their toll and, irrespective of the weather, a not-too-strenuous route is more often than not the order of the day.

The first day of 1980 stands out as one of those occasions. We couldn't have hoped for better conditions. From the moment we woke and watched the first rays of the winter sun slant across the snow-clad slopes around the head of Borrowdale we knew that we must be in for a day of dreams, no matter where we walked. In fact, we chose to drive out of Borrowdale and on to Braithwaite for an ascent of Grisedale Pike and some of its neighbours. A late start, combined with several delicate heads and a slow, leisurely pace were the reasons why we had only covered the three miles to the summit by lunch-time, but what a place that was to take a break for food. Sitting in the sun beside the cairn we revelled in our situation. Beyond the distant Vale of Eden and

dominated by the extensive plateau of Cross Fell, reared the white scarp of the northern Pennines while behind us, across the sparkling waters of the Solway Firth, the little visited Galloway and Moffat hills were snow-bound from head to toe. With views stretching from the Pennines to southern Scotland, as well as over most of winter Lakeland, we were more than content with our lot.

Despite the bright sun the air was intensely cold. Our sandwiches were consumed rapidly before we pushed on, along the lofty snow ridge, to Hopegill Head and views of a softer, greener landscape around the coast of Cumbria. There was insufficient time to complete the horseshoe circuit of Coledale so we satisfied ourselves instead with the airy ridge walk out to Whiteside from where we looked into the shadowed depths around Loweswater and Crummock Water — the gathering dusk a reminder that the day was drawing to a close. Daylight was fading fast as we retraced our steps to Hopegill Head, the sun sinking quickly towards the sea. Lengthening shadows chased us down to Coledale Hause and the path leading to the mine road that would take us back to the village. In near darkness we sauntered along the easy gravel track and felt the frost nibble at cheeks and fingers. Directly ahead rose Blencathra and, as we watched, a huge full moon eased itself above the crest and the valleys were once more aglow. Could there have been a more perfect way to end this lovely winter's day spent wandering the high snow ridges of Lakeland?

The monotonous western flanks of the Helvellyn range and their various routes of ascent are the quickest means of reaching the high ridges from a winter base in Borrowdale. Valuable time is easily lost by driving all the way round to Patterdale and not infrequently the road via Troutbeck and Dockray is impassable, as we discovered on the one occasion we attempted an approach of the mountain from the Ullswater side. At New Year then, we usually climb from Thirlspot or Stanah and at this time I would not dare refer to these slopes as monotonous or uninteresting. Under full winter conditions they take on an entirely different character.

My most remarkable New Year ascent of Helvellyn was a quiet sunny day several years ago when sharp distant views and a magnificent sunset were the prizes we

A break for lunch on January snows (Peter Wilson).

Above *On a clear January day the Pennines are clearly visible from Helvellyn* (Peter Wilson).

Right *Helvellyn trig point* (Peter Wilson).

collected for the effort of a ten mile walk. It was also the day we came to respect the smooth hill-slopes that rise above the A591.

We parked the car at Stanah with some difficulty. Black ice covered the small parking area and necessitated man-handling the vehicle into position. Soft deep snow smothered the fields and fellside above Thirlspot and we could only guess at where the path might be. We struggled up, taking turns to break trail and stopping often to regain breath and admire the improving views towards Keswick and Skiddaw. Eventually we sighted cairns. The snow was thinning and where the gradient eased and the path traversed towards Helvellyn Gill we stepped from snow on to clear water-ice.

This was bad news: we had ice-axes but had failed to bring crampons and it was the latter we needed now. Gingerly we edged our way across, kicking hard with the boots wherever we thought we could gain adequate grip and meandering from one grassy tuft to another. At one stage we all went down with an almighty thump but were none the worse for the experience. A ramp of frozen snow replaced the ice on the steep slope beside Browncove

Crags and carried the tracks of a recent skier. Again we regretted the lack of crampons, but using old footsteps and cutting new ones where needed we were soon up to the gentler ground above the crags.

From here it was a mere stroll to the summit, the hills were bare of snow — the gales a few days previous having swept it down to lower levels. Our topsy-turvy views of white snow-filled dales and brown hill tops ranged from Pendle Hill in Lancashire to many miles beyond the Scottish border. With the sun beating down and a panorama of glowing hills we agreed that there was no better place to be on such a day as this.

To complete our walk we turned north and followed the high ground, crossing Whiteside, Raise, Stybarrow Dodd and Watson's Dodd before fading light forced us to descend. Wending down from the cairn on Watson's Dodd the sun and cloud combined in spectacular manner and produced a long playing symphony of colour. A rich orange sky alternated with gold-rimmed bands of steely-grey cloud with the sun appearing and disappearing as it dropped further towards the sea. Night crept silently down over the fells

Snow covered approach to the summit of Skiddaw (David Palmer).

Above *The snow line on Skiddaw is clearly visible from Grisedale Pike on this January day* (Peter Wilson).

Right *A January mackerel sky over Helvellyn Lower Man as seen from Whiteside* (Peter Wilson).

Above right *Ice-blasted snow on Hindscarth* (Peter Wilson).

and the frost regained its grip on the January land. We slithered across the lethal ice-bound fields above the Thirlmere aqueduct and once more wished we had carried crampons. The dull grassy slopes of Helvellyn had taught us a lesson we would remember but the fells had also shared with us their treasures and for that we were grateful.

Skiddaw has been curiously omitted during most of our New Year visits to Lakeland — only once having been the main objective. This neglect probably stems from the difficulty of obtaining sufficient mileage from it to fill even a short winter's day. Consequently, it is an ideal hill to tackle on the first day of a new year, when enthusiasm requires that a high peak must be reached and yet only a minimum of energy can be summoned. Undoubtedly the finest way to ascend Skiddaw is along the Ullock Pike-Carl Side ridge, ending with a formidable 700 ft climb of the loose screes that surround the long narrow summit. This is the way we went on another January morning.

Labouring under the added weight of ice axes and crampons this time we picked our way across the frozen pastures towards the base of Ullock Pike. The Herdwick sheep looked more bemused than usual by the layer of white hoar-frost that had ruined their

breakfast, but the rumble of a distant tractor had them charging towards the field gate in eager anticipation of more nourishing fodder. Hard weather for sheep and farmers is often ideal for hill-walking, especially when the sun shines down on the great frosty silence that settles over the fells.

Snow-covered ground became more abundant the higher we climbed and our ice-axes were soon in use as the angle steepened. From below, Ullock Pike appears as a prominent peak with the land falling away sharply on all sides. It may come as a disappointment then, on reaching the summit, to find it is no more than the termination of a long tapering ridge that suddenly drops towards Bassenthwaite. Yet it was elation rather than disappointment that greeted us that day as we moved out of shadow into the sun to see spread before us ridge after ridge of gleaming white hills fading into the far distance.

We passed swiftly along the corniced ridge to Longside Edge and Carl Side. In the tiny depression before Skiddaw we fixed crampons then stamped up the frozen snow to meet the raw east wind that quickly found every chink in our armour and penetrated to the very core. The summit view indicator and cairn were half

Taking shelter from the wind behind a wall on Helvellyn (Peter Wilson).

buried by drifted snow. Crude seats were hurriedly fashioned in the lee of the cairn and we flopped down, thankful to be protected from the numbing wind. The weather forecast had mentioned temperatures of −9°C at 3,000 ft and we can confirm that it was mighty cold.

Fortified by hot drinks and sweet food we prepared to flee this Arctic environment and the north-west shoulder was our line of descent. Once clear of the upper ice-field we removed crampons and by a combined standing and sitting glissade swooped down the long crusty snow slopes to the beck in Southerndale in a fraction of the time it had taken us to ascend.

We had been out for less than five hours but were well satisfied with our modest achievement. There can surely be no finer way of starting the year than by striding out across the frozen fell-tops with unforgettable views to far horizons.

Not all my January days in the fells of Lakeland

are associated with sunshine on the snows and perfect visibility. On numerous occasions snow has been lacking and the hills shrouded in a warm, damp mist that ensured we steamed inside our waterproofs and saw nothing of the surrounding countryside. There have been other days when perhaps we shouldn't have gone out and still others when we didn't. These wild days of wind and rain reveal the force of the elements and serve as a warning not to take the hills too lightly in winter. We have often returned to the valleys soaked to the skin (despite modern shell garments) and having been blasted by the gales. A pointless exercise you may think, but we have never failed to feel invigorated, having tested the elements and been tested by them. If we hadn't gone we would never have known.

We once took heed of a poor weather forecast and lowered our sights from the craggy Borrowdale fells to the smoother, gentler terrain above the sleepy hamlet of Mungrisedale. The three hills — Bowscale Fell, Bannerdale Crags and Souther Fell — would, we thought, be ample on such a nasty day. We drove the distance and parked but there was no way we were going to get up the hills. The rain rattled on the windscreens and frequent, violent gusts rocked our cars. We feared we would be blown away if we ventured out. The fleshpots of Keswick were a more popular choice for whiling away such a wild and filthy day.

Days when we didn't set out have been few and far between though. Vile conditions have nearly always been attacked in the hope of later improvement but rarely have such hopes been justified and route modification is often required to avoid the worst of the weather. Over the years several attempts to reach the summit of Great Gable have been thwarted by lashing rain and gales. Beck Head, or thereabouts, has been the setting for two of these forced retreats. On both occasions we approached from the top of Honister Pass, along the Moses Trod path, and were afforded

relative shelter from the raging south-westerly by the bulk of Gable and Kirk Fell. Not until we had stuck our heads around the corner overlooking Beck Head did we realize the full might of the weather.

The first time this happened we had managed to struggle some distance up the screes towards Gable when an unexpected gust bowled some people over and the rest of us clung together for fear of being blown clean across the valley to Haystacks. We knew we were beaten and hastily returned to the comparative calm below Gable Crag. The second time was a day we had originally earmarked for Pillar but as we followed the easily graded track, high above Ennerdale, the rain increased in intensity so we reduced our objective to Kirk Fell. At Beck Head we were pelted by horizontal sleet driven with such force that we could not face into it for more than a couple of seconds at a time. All idea of Kirk Fell was abandoned and we also dismissed

Great Gable and Pillar, tall against the skyline (Peter Wilson).

Gable. It was not a day to go any further on the fells. We scurried along the narrow north traverse path, directly beneath Gable Crag, and found temporary respite from the evil weather. In Windy Gap, once more assailed by the stinging sleet, we decided to ignore even Green Gable, though only a five minute walk away. We ran down the pink screes to rejoin Moses Trod, anxious only to return to Honister, and the shelter and warmth of the car, as quickly as possible.

Green Gable saw the end of another attempt on its higher neighbour when a combination of greasy rocks, torrential rain and half a gale caused one of our number to tumble and gash his head on the sharp stones. Neat and tidy first aid was impossible, plaster and tape would not stick in the wet, so a pad of lint held in place by a woollen hat had to suffice. The casualty was able to descend so we went down by Aaron Slack to Styhead and on to Seathwaite. Three stitches were inserted in the wound at Keswick Hospital. Although only a

minor incident it served to show that the wild wet days demand respect: wind and rain on the hills are forces to be reckoned with. Temperature inversions can occur frequently during the autumn and winter months when atmospheric pressure is high and there is little wind. On clear frosty nights progressive chilling of air near ground level causes it to sink to low levels within valleys, forming dense fog banks. The morning sun gradually evaporates these valley clouds but often the inversion persists all day. Walkers who venture onto high ridges at such times are rewarded for their efforts by days of unbroken sunshine, with the crisp air burning on the face and the hills soaring supremely out of a silent white world of valley mists.

Most of my inversion days have occurred on Lakeland hills and although years have passed and similar conditions met with a dozen times or more, the first occasion I broke out of the cloud, and witnessed the magic stillness that only winter can bring, remains special to me.

Far left *From Esk House, Great and Green Gable reveal their winter grandeur* (Peter Wilson).

Left *This winter's afternoon Dunnerdale and Seathwaite are visible and the coastline just discernible on the horizon beyond. The viewpoint is from the path to Crinkle Crags* (Eric Whitehead).

During a Christmas and New Year vacation from university I obtained work in a Grasmere hotel, hoping for time off to explore the fells. It was not to be, however, and only after New Year, when trade had slackened, did the opportunity to climb some hills arise. On the day prior to my return to academia I seized the chance of a free afternoon and dashed out. It was a depressing day with fog down to street level but I was keen for fresh air and exercise so directed my feet towards the beck of Greenhead Gill and the steep unrelenting slopes of Stone Arthur.

I climbed hard and fast through dead, tangled bracken and burst out from this twilight world just before reaching the rocky tor crowning the summit. On top I gaped in disbelief at what I saw. No one had told me that January could put on a spectacle such as this, I was bewitched. A smooth carpet of cloud had been laid across Lakeland for my benefit, concealing everything below the 1,500 ft contour. The high fells rose sharp and clear, reflecting in their bright hues of red, brown and grey a warmth and intensity I had not thought possible from a winter sun. For some time I could only sit engrossed by this feast of colour. The hills were resplendent, resting like sleek yachts at anchor in a sea of foaming white beneath the bright blue heavens.

With sunset still an hour away I continued along the easy-angled shoulder to Greatrigg Man. The extra height improved the panorama, which now included an unfamiliar broadside view of Striding Edge with the cone of Catstycam peeping up beyond. I reached Heron Pike as the sun began to drop behind the silhouette of the Coniston fells. For a moment after it had gone the hills were rimmed with gold, then a flush of fiery orange light filled the skies and the heavens blazed as day gave way to night. In the half-light I arrived at Alcock Tarn and located the path winding down to Grasmere. The valley clouds were freezing hard and frost feathers grew from my hair and eyebrows as I descended.

Winter clouds break against Great and Green Gable (Peter Wilson).

I had waited almost two weeks for a day on the fells but I doubt if any other day could have been as satisfying as these few short hours had been. Such, perhaps, are the rewards for patience.

For a few years in succession we always made a point of returning to the Lake District in the middle of January and were fortunate to strike gold on each occasion. After spending New Year near the head of Borrowdale we preferred to walk the eastern fells above Patterdale or the southern fells around Langdale and Coniston on these weekend visits. It was the Coniston hills this time that provided me with such a stunning temperature inversion that I still rate that day, almost ten years ago now, as one of my most memorable Lakeland days. What began as an unexceptional

winter's morning in a northern industrial town ninety miles away ended in a similar manner in a quiet Lakeland village, but for several hours in between we were in a different world — a world far removed from the dreary still greyness that had clamped down firmly over Lancashire and Cumbria—a world of dazzling sunshine, of rich brown hill tops streaked with snow and of an ocean of cotton-wool cloud gently lapping the glowing fell-sides.

A late start and a two-hour drive put paid to most of the morning so it was well after mid-day as we approached the top of Wetherlam. Snow still choked the Hen Crag gullies although there was little to speak of on the ridge itself. We had been swathed in mist from the outset and the summit seemed a cheerless

we raced the final hundred feet to the summit of Swirl How.

For several minutes we stood in silence, totally captivated by the scenes that confronted us. When we eventually spoke it was in hushed tones lest we should wake from our dream. But this was no fantasy and soon we were yelling with delight at all we saw. The entire Lake District and the miles beyond were buried by a blanket of soft rippled cloud reaching up to a height of about 2,500 ft, while thrusting skyward through this white and fleecy cloak were those hills of greater altitude. Near at hand, across the unseen gulf of Wrynose Bottom, rose the upper snow-splashed crags of the Scafells and Bowfell. The long swelling ridges of Fairfield and Helvellyn broke through on the north-east horizon and eighteen miles north the unmistakable tops of Skiddaw and Blencathra floated as isolated and mystic islands on the ocean of cloud.

We wandered about the summit absorbing this lavish display of Lakeland pageantry and recording it on film. As we stood on the rim of Greenburn our shadows, magnified many times over, extended several tens of metres across the cloud. These were the fabled 'Brocken Spectres' of which we had read but never before witnessed. Around the head of each shadow a small circular rainbow was visible — the halo or glory that often accompanies the Spectre.

During the time we spent on Swirl How, other hills began to shake off the rolling cloud and poke their summits into the still bright air. Great Carrs was first to emerge, shortly followed by Grey Friar. The ridge south, to Brim Fell and Coniston Old Man, couldn't quite make up its mind what to do but as we turned and walked in that direction it finally slipped free, head and shoulders now held proud, and began to shine in warm tints of brown and grey. Cloud was spilling across the ridge at Levers Hause, where we were temporarily forced to leave our world of dazzling sunlight. Back in the sun on Brim Fell we watched Wetherlam, our first summit, discard its mantle of white and, miles beyond, we identified the highest summits of the High Street ridge.

The Old Man of Coniston was our last top so we lingered long, basking in the sunshine and still unable to believe it was really happening. To the south, as far as the eye could see, stretched an unbroken sheet of pure white

place at which to linger but, as we rested by the cairn, a sudden distinct brightening and a large ragged hole torn in the clouds gave us a glimpse of blue sky above and a hint of what might follow. We waited in vain. The blue disappeared then proceeded to reappear at intervals of a few minutes, but always overhead, denying us the far-reaching views we longed for. If Wetherlam had been just fifty feet higher it could have been so very different.

Time was passing and other hills had yet to be climbed. We departed Wetherlam, exasperated by its half-hearted attempts to cast off its misty veil, and descended back into the thick of things to Swirl Hause. High on the rocky ridge of Prison Band we once again experienced increasing overhead brightness and blueness and almost before we had realized it we had stepped clean out of the cloud and into warm sunshine. The transformation was abrupt and dramatic and

Top left *Scafell Pike and Great Gable viewed from Grey Knotts* (Peter Wilson).

Below left *This view of Great Carrs through a telephoto lens was taken from Hell Gill Pike. The flanks of Coniston Old Man are on the left, Goats House and Dow Crag to the right* (Eric Whitehead).

Left *Wetherlam and Low Water from Coniston Old Man: a snowy coating highlights the ice carved and shaped relief of much of the Lake District* (Lynn Williams).

corrugated cloud hiding the forests of Grisedale, the estuaries of the rivers Leven and Duddon and the shifting sands of Morecambe Bay. The north country was well and truly obscured, only the high fells had escaped and only those who had chanced to climb them would have cause to remember this day.

As the sun dipped below the western horizon we prepared to descend. One final look at this supreme cloudscape revealed a tiny rock turret just behind the northern shoulder of Dow Crag. A walker standing on the topmost rocks of Eskdale's Harter Fell would see the sunset after all while the cloud swirled around his feet. Shortly after leaving the cairn we re-entered the murk and with darkness fast approaching made our way through the abandoned quarry workings, past Low Water and on to the village. Street lamps were lit and car headlights pierced the fog, as they had done all day. The contrast was immense. Nature had chosen to enthral us and, appropriately humbled, we had returned to the land of men and daily life.

Few people, if any, have ever sung the praises of Lakeland's central ridge that runs north from the Langdale Pikes and terminates abruptly some nine miles distant at the easily remembered height of Walla Crag (1,234 ft) overlooking Keswick and Derwentwater. The stretch from Ullscarf to Bleaberry Fell comes in for much choice comment from Wainwright, and justly so; 'wear thigh-length gumboots', 'not a walk to be undertaken for pleasure', and 'a walk to wish on one's worst enemy' give some idea of his feelings about the place. For much of the year the ridge assumes the properties of a vast sponge, soaking up the Lakeland rain and reluctant to release it, save perhaps through the lower clothing of those attempting to cross it. The Irish have a neat phrase that sums it up perfectly — 'turf floating on water'. An ideal place then, on most occasions, to assess the water-repellant qualities of the multitude of boot dressings and proofings.

Choose the right sort of January day though, as we did some years ago, when a rock-hard frost had gripped the fells in its iron fist and a light dusting of snow sparkled beneath a dazzling sun, and I guarantee that wet feet will be the least of your worries. Crossing the frozen bogs gives you a freedom that is usually lacking here — to enjoy the surrounding scenery rather than having to look to every step.

We began by climbing to Castle Head, a low wooded knob of volcanic rock guarding the Borrowdale road. Thin fog hung amongst the knarled branches but the summit was clear and the air bright and crisp. We arrived to watch the morning mists melt silently away and reveal the flat glassy calm of Derwentwater. Across the vale in uniformed array of white snow cap and russet bracken waistcoat soared Catbells, Causey and Grisedale Pike looking twice their measured height. We had begun with a truly magnificent start to the day and there was more to come.

As we gained height the sun gained strength. Anoraks, gloves and hats were packed away, sleeves rolled up and stockings pushed down. The easy slopes to Walla Crag had us wiping the perspiration from our eyes and perhaps we would rather not recall our language on the final steep rise to Bleaberry Fell, but a few

Right *Cold January: this is Eskdale and Bowfell rising into stormclouds beyond* (Simon Wilkinson).

Above right *High Street from Helvellyn* (Peter Wilson).

moments later, as we reached the sturdy cairn, the clammy discomforts of the past hour of climbing were instantly forgotten. Before us, instead of a deep valley complete with reservoir and plantations of larch and spruce, a golden ribbon of cloud twisted away into the distance and through the gap of Dunmail Raise. We marvelled at our good fortune, high up amongst the snows with the sun smiling down from a cloudless blue sky and a glorious and mysterious temperature inversion clearly evident. Down below on the main Thirlmere road motorists would doubtless be crawling along, attempting to penetrate the gloom with headlights dipped and frustrations mounting.

High above them we danced along the broad ridge to High Seat and High Tove, skating on the frozen pools and kicking up the snow as we went, until coming down the hill we descended joyously into Watendlath, already deep in shadow. Smoke curled lazily from the farmhouse chimneys and the only sound was the crunch of boots on thin ice and gravel. Climbing quickly over the fell to Rosthwaite, we saw the last orange streaks of the dying sun and sensed the frost tightening its hold over the earth. Privileged to share its beauty in this way, we could only acknowledge that once more Lakeland had woven within us its very special January magic.

Peter Wilson began hill-walking during his school days in Nelson, Lancashire. Whilst at university he spent vacations leading walking groups for the Countrywide Holidays Association (CHA) at their centres throughout Britain. He now lectures in the Department of Environmental Studies at the University of Ulster, Coleraine and continues his hill-walking at every opportunity. His other interests include cross-country skiing and landscape photography and he has contributed articles on walking to *The Great Outdoors, Climber, Footloose* and *Cumbria*.

February: In search of song and an early spring

CAMERON McNEISH

Rain lashing the city from early morning had cleared the winter streets of shoppers. A pre-dawn gloom loitered in the sky and refused to budge. The statues in St Stephen's Green were truly drenched, and the railings dripped with water. Occasionally someone would scurry past me, a tormented haste borne of the desire to be somewhere warm and dry. I'd never seen Dublin streets so quiet. I missed the music of Dublin. Instead of the drone and squeal of Uillean pipes at the corner of Grafton Street there was only the slush of traffic on drenched roads. Where penny whistles normally crooned Irish airs on O'Connel Bridge there was only the drip of water into the Liffey. Old Anna Liffey, the soul of Dublin, swollen by the tears of her town.

It was brighter in the pub, with an air of conviviality. Too early for the music session to start though and the barman had time to blether.

'Sure it's a bitch of a day and not for good people to be out and about.'

I agreed with him and ordered a hot whiskey.

'And what brings you to Ireland?' he asked, recognizing my lack of brogue. 'You over on business?'

'Yes, partly', I answered. 'Business and pleasure. I'm hoping to do a bit of walking in Wicklow and Kerry, and maybe Connemara.' I suspected that answer would have some impact.

'Holy Mother of Jesus,' he blurted, 'Are ye daft or somethin' — going climbing mountains at this time o' the year? Kerry's a great place right enough, but she can be a real bitch when she wants to be, especially at this time o' the year.'

I retreated to a table by the window and left him shaking his head. It was an odd time to take a walking trip in Ireland, but beggars can't be chosers and since I was primarily in Ireland to collect some material for a radio programme on ancient Irish mythology and early music I had decided to visit some favourite hill places

as well. The fact that it was February hadn't worried me unduly. I knew that with a bit of luck I would be swopping the snowy fastness of Scotland's February hills with the early spring of Gulf Stream Ireland. I expected crocuses, daffodils, curlews and peewits...

> The bog is like the raven's dress, the loud cuckoo makes greeting, the speckled fish leaps, mighty is the swift warrior. Man thrives, the maiden flourishes in her fine strong prime: every wood is fair from crest to ground, fair each great goodly field. Delightful is the season's splendour, rough winter has gone; bright is every fertile wood...

The optimism of spring, but was I being too optimistic? I rubbed a clear patch in the fog that clouded the window and peered out. The rain had stopped, the shoppers had returned, and soon the pipers and the fiddlers would grace their traditional stances on Grafton Street and O'Connel Bridge. Ould Dublin smiled and Anna Liffey's tears dried up.

Due to the not dissimilar passions of the Irish, music and mountains, I had come to know Ireland and love her. The music of Clare, the rugged hills of Kerry, the emptiness of Connemara and the tales of Fionn and Oisin had captivated me and rarely a year goes by that doesn't see me swoop in on Dublin town after the short air hop from Glasgow or roll off the car ferry at Dun Laoghaire.

Ireland is shaped like a great saucer, the mountains of the coast forming a great bowl of the central plains. Only between the counties of Louth and Meath, north of Dublin, is there a break in the mountain ring. In a sense this is an over simplification of the truth but there is enough validity in it for a walker.

South of Dublin lie the Wicklow hills whose outliers can be seen from the city's streets. These great sprawling domes attract walkers at weekends in the summer, but tend to be quiet at other times, a refreshing and purifying change from busy Lakeland and North Wales. Like Scotland's Cairngorms the real interest of the Wicklows isn't so much in the rounded tops as the glacier scoured valleys — Glenmacnass, Glenmalure and Glendalough, glens of ancient history. The big hills of the Wicklows, Mullaghcleevaun and Tonelegee, bow before the only 3,000 footer of the area, Lugnaquilia, 3,039 ft above sea level.

As I drove out of Dublin towards my hotel in Lucan the late afternoon gloaming was momentarily lightened by a break in the heavy grey sky. Towards the west, the clouds were rent by stray sun-glow, weak, but real enough as the limp rays broke across the country to light up the Dublin mountains. I took it as a good sign to head for Wicklow and a winter, or early spring meeting with Lugnaquilia. I hoped to stay with some good friends in Kilkenny, and planned a quick sortie with Lug' before driving southwards again. Jim keeps a good bottle and is a grand lad with the tales so I was in fine fettle for a good night to follow the day. As it happened the day was pretty good too.

I left the car in Glenmalure on a morning that had been well washed by the rains of the previous day. My disappointment at seeing little sign of spring raiment was soon lost in the vibrancy of the morning. There were even snow wreaths high on the steep slopes above Carrawaystick Brook.

A barking raven kept me company as I sweated up the zig-zag path beyond the Avonbeg River. A small ruin lay on the ridge at the top of the zig-zags and I stopped to take off some clothes. A strange place for a building and I wondered if it could have been an old sheiling as we have in Scotland. More likely the ruins represented the remains of a shepherd's hut, for there was an old farm in the glen below. We become used to finding ruins all over the highlands of Scotland, but Ireland didn't suffer the atrocities of the clearances or at least not in the same way. Ireland's history is bloodthirsty enough though — similar clan feuding, then famines due to the potato blight, terrible landownership largely due to foreign landlords, and, as one writer succinctly put it, 'ecclesiastical interference'. Despite that, it's still a land that is largely lived in and as such, offers a very different hill experience from Scotland.

The 'go-back, go-back, go-back' cackle of grouse made me feel at home, as did the clagging heather. I knew that there should be a path somewhere on the Glenmalure side of the hill and it was by luck more than good navigation that I found it. I'm glad I did, for it made the walking much easier and soon I was striding out, enjoying the openness of these high moors. There's a lot of Scotland in those high Wicklows, and a bit of Derbyshire too as you fight your way through peat hags which stand five or six feet in height. The previous day's rain had left its legacy and my feet, despite well-proofed boots and gaiters, were soon sodden. I didn't mind too much as I didn't have far to go; on to the upland plateau which goes by the name of Percy's Table, and then up to the summit itself, the least interesting part of the hill.

It was too early to head back to the car, so I wandered north to have a look at the North Prison, a high corrie whose cliffs are said to hold good snow and ice in winter. Indeed there was still a lot of snow plastering the crag. Snow and ice climbing isn't something we normally associate with Ireland but I know some of the Dublin lads get some good sport in the Wicklows in cold winters.

The return walk to Glenmalure was uneventful, and my thoughts wandered into planning the rest of my walks for the next week or so. I'd decided that I probably wouldn't have time to do anything in Connemara for I had a fair bit of work to get through in County Clare, of all the Gaeltacht areas the finest for collecting traditional music. But I couldn't have a week in Ireland and not visit Kerry. County Kerry, where I would stay with the Doonans, grand Gaelic speaking people who had a fund of good songs and stories of the Fianna. My journey was planned. Tonight Kilkenny, tomorrow Killorglin, County Kerry, and the next day Carrauntoohill, the highest mountain in Ireland.

There must be a word for the area of land where softness and harshness come together. The Gaelic probably has it, for that ancient language is so much more expressive than our own, and in Ireland, particularly in Kerry, there is more interplay between these two states than anywhere else I have seen. Look down on the counterpane of fields from the rocky slopes of MacGillycuddy's Reeks. There is no landward 'machair' here, only the thin dividing line of an old drystone dyke separating the rich green from the rugged

Right *Carrauntoohill, the highest hill in Ireland* (Cameron McNeish).

Far right *Loch Acoose and McGillycuddy's Reeks, Kerry* (Cameron McNeish).

browns and ochres of the lower slopes.

Kerry landowners of the past have wrestled with a wild landscape to scourge every inch of uncompromising soil from the possession of the great hills that dominate them. The effect is one of great charm, for the hillwalker gets the impression of being in a living landscape rather than a desert, where the reek of turf smoke can be sensed high above the patchwork below and occasionally even the drone of voices may be heard, lifted by thermals to the topmost crags of the hills themselves.

One has to be blessed to experienced these sensations, blessed by uncharacteristic calm and dry weather which is not common in this land where life is so often dominated by the great troughs of depression which are spawned out in the anonymity of the vast Atlantic swells. To a person raised and nurtured on the unpeopled highlands of Scotland, where the only sign of human habitation in the glens is more often than not in the bony skeletons of ruined shielings, such an interchange between wild and tamed is both novel and quite delightful.

Lying, trying to attract what there was of a weak spring sunshine, beside a hawthorn bush which was alive with the sound of chattering tiny wrens, it is easy to tumble back into the time when this land was dominated by those who are now folk heroes. Down below by Glencar, lies the spot where the bold Ossian, bardic son of the renowned Fionn MacCumhail or Fingal as he is recognized in Scotland, returned to the land of the living after reputedly spending 300 years in Tir-Nan-Og, the Land of the Ever Young. It was here that he searched for his Fianna brothers, celebrated in mountain and glen names in all the Celtic lands.

Even further back the land was peopled by the mysterious Tuatha De Danaan, a strange and cultured folk who may have been wanderers from Sicily, Sardinia, Italy and Spain, the ancient Tartessia, or were they figments of a Celtic imagination? Could it be that the great mountain that rose behind me, Carauntoohill, or Corran Tuathuill, the highest in all Ireland, was named after these Tuatha De Danaan people? The thought appealed to me. The hill of the faery folk, for it was the De Danaan who were the archetypal faery people. Their ways were mysterious to the Celts who occupied Erin on their arrival. Their culture, it seems was significantly more advanced than the Celts and they surrounded themselves with an aura of magic. The magic people, the Faery Folk, Tuatha De Danaan.

There certainly was an aura of magic around their mountain this hazy springlike day. I was prompted from my daydreaming into activity. The days were still short and there was work to be done. The softness of the scene was about to become harsher, as harsh as anything in the British hills.

A horseshoe of high rugged hills rose sheer from a figure-of-eight lough held deep in their bosom. From the shores of that lough the rocky walls rose to a jagged skyline, steep walls, seared and riven by scree runnels and prominent ribs of sandstone. The shape of the cliffs, together with the great height of them, created an atmosphere not unlike that of an immense cathedral. The contrast between the mountain savagery and the pastoral softness of the earlier scene left me awed, breathless and excited, and impatient to get to grips with the tight ridges which enclose this Coomloughra Horseshoe of Carrauntoohill.

I grew hot as I made my ungainly way up loose scree towards the ridge crest which leads to Caher, the fort, at 3,250 ft. By the time I reached the first of the three summits the watery sunshine took a tangible form, a thin drizzle hung in the air like a veil. I was glad to crawl into the tiny stone structure which

Above *Carrauntoohill, on the left, from Caher* (Cameron McNeish).

Right *From the opposite direction: Caher from Carrauntoohill, Kerry* (Cameron McNeish).

perches there. The latter day pilgrim who built this remote oratory was certainly not concerned with physical comfort. I couldn't help but recall the words of a tenth century Irish poem, describing the basic hut of a hermit priest:

> 'The size of my hut, small yet not small, a place of familiar paths; the she-bird in its dress of blackbird colour sings a melodious strain from its gable.
> 'The stags of Druim Rolach leap out of its stream of trim meadows; from them red Roighne can be seen, noble Mucraimhe and Maenmhagh.
> 'A little hidden lowly hut, which owns the paths which you may reach; you will not go with me to see it, but I shall tell of it.'

Carrauntoohill from the Caher ridge with the mist clouding, 'reeking', up the slope (Hamish Brown).

After this first summit of Caher the going becomes steeper. Tracings of a track run down to a high col, then steeply up to the real summit, before winding a tormented zig-zag towards the south-west ridge of Carrauntoohill.

The immediate approaches to this ridge offer easy walking on good springy turf, giving an eagle's eye view of the rest of these unlikely-named MacGillycuddy's Reeks. The great coums, or corries, split the hills into a series of high, ridge-linked peaks, looking higher than their 3,000 ft would suggest against the flat plains of Mid-Kerry and Cork. To the north a great finger of land thrusts its way out across the dark waters of Dingle Bay, reaching out, stretching into the Atlantic. Close to the end of that finger, like an afterthought, rises the bulk of Brandon, Brandon of the blessed. To my Celt-sodden mind it is certainly the most atmospheric of mountains in whose brooding corrie bowels dwell the legend of the banshee,

Above *Looking across Dingle Bay to the wide sweep of the Atlantic* (Cameron McNeish).

Left *The summit of Carrauntoohill, like many Irish mountains, carries a great emblem of faith* (Cameron McNeish).

Top left *Looking into Coomloughra from the summit ridge of Caher* (Cameron McNeish).

Bottom left *Looking towards the McGillycuddy Reeks from the Carrauntoohill/Beenkeragh col* (Cameron McNeish).

the little people, and the finest of all the Fingalian tales, a bubbling pot of lore and legend, a place where one may dream unashamably and where the simple strum of a harp could bring tears streaming down one's face like the waters of its Paternoster Lakes. A remarkable mountain, to be sure.

The flat-topped summit of Carrauntoohill, some 3,414 ft above the Atlantic, is, like Brandon, a strangely humbling place. A huge cross stands here, a boxed metal construction of a thing which even in its rusting and dilapidated condition does not fail to register a holy presence. Even on this grey day of Irish softness this great Christian emblem cast its aura of peace and grace across the entire scene, its very presence in such a place re-emphasizing the wonder of God's creation and the base beauty of it which we so often take for granted. I was glad of the cross.

Like an ecstatic evangelist I left the summit of Carrauntoohill behind me leaping from rock to rock until the narrow Arran-like ridge to Beenkeragh stopped me dead in my tracks. I had been here before. Several years ago, on my first visit to Kerry, I had wandered on to this ridge and on to a steep scramble which led to rocky walls and great drops. I made sure I didn't make the error again. I believe this is the spot where most of Ireland's mountain accidents take place, with about twenty people dying in the past thirty years. Care is required.

The arete runs northwards for about three-quarters of a mile to a col which lies on the 3,000 ft contour, a col which offers superb crag-framed views into Beenkeragh's hidden loch and corrie, and across the wilds of the Hags Glen to the other hills of the Reeks. All the guidebooks suggest that there are sheep tracks which, if found, skirt the worst (or the best — it depends how you look at such things) of the ridge. I couldn't find them. Not that I searched for them particularly hard, for there is nothing finer than a good scramble on coarse rock. As I scrambled the rocky jumble of slab and block, the watery sun appeared again lighting up the corrie below with an ochrous glow. Despite the wetness of the rock, and the coldness of it on my bare hands, I enjoyed the rocky thrill of the scramble, tip-toeing along the crest, searching out the simplest line over the rocky jumble. I could easily have been on the rocky ridges of A'Chir or Beinn Tarsuinn in Arran, or on the best of the Aonach Eagach or even the Cuillin itself,

such was the thrill of the ridge. Who wants to follow sheep tracks when there are scrambles like this on offer? A rough boulder field separates the end of the ridge from Beenkeragh's summit, the Peak of the Sheep at 3,314 ft, an anticlimax after the exertions of the ridge. The remaining walk to Skregmore, the final top of the horseshoe, looked fairly dull, a bit like having to watch the B movie after enjoying the main one.

Needless to say, like many minor summits, it offered the best view of the day, a grand panorama of the group as a whole. The entire ridgeline appears serrated and rugged with plunging precipices dropping into the great scooped cauldron that holds the loughs, and above all, a sky that was now smiling, the only hint of benevolence left in the whole scene. But within half an hour I was back in the soft country and I lingered to enjoy the last of the winter daylight. The lowing of cattle sounded close and I could smell the turf smoke in the air once more. I began to look forward to Mrs Doolin's soda scones.

The village of Dingle is one of contrasts, old Ireland living uncomfortably with the new. Donkeys and jaunting cars are common, and in season the commercial interests of tourism tend to jar. I was thankful it was February. 'Who wants to go to Dingle in February?' I had overheard someone ask in the pub in Killorglin the night before. Well, I had two reasons: to climb Brandon, one of the finest mountains in the British Isles and to experience the delights of a seafood meal in Doyle's, a restaurant world-famous for its fruits of the sea.

But I was to be disappointed. Doyle's was shut and I had to make do with a bar meal in the hotel. It wasn't the greatest of food but that didn't matter too much for I believe that Guinness is both food and drink to a hungry man and I had enough to feed a regiment later on in Flaherty's Bar, a grand place for music. Flaherty's is a bit of an institution in Dingle, and some years before I had been enjoying the music there when a little slip of a man wheedled his way up beside me and whispered, 'How are ye Matt me bhoy? Will ye give us a tune?'

'Pardon', said I, a bit put out.

'Come on Matt, give us a tune. If ye don't have yer flute with ya, one o' the lads'll lend you theirs.'

Left January: *As we traverse the Whitestones route of Helvellyn, Skiddaw stands proud on the skyline beyond* (Peter Wilson).

Below January: *Coniston Fells can seem to stretch forever* (Peter Wilson).

Right February: *The view from Brandon mountain to the Stradbally Mountains, looking along the line of the Paternoster Lakes* (Hamish Brown).

Below February: *Carrauntoohill and Beenkeragh, the highest mountains in Ireland with cloud 'reeking' around their summits* (Hamish Brown).

Top right March: *Early spring in Lathkill Dale in the White Peak is best enjoyed on foot* (Richard Gilbert).

Bottom right March: *Further north in the Pennines, snow remains on the high ground near Bodesbeck Law* (Richard Gilbert).

Above March: *On a descent from the summit of Hart Crag in the Lake District, small snow patches are still to be seen* (Richard Gilbert).

Below March: *From Beinn an Eoin (an outlier of Ben More Coigach) the view on a warm March day is magnificent* (Richard Gilbert).

On any visit to Dingle, Doyle's fish restaurant welcomes the traveller (Hamish Brown).

'I think you're mistaking me for someone else.' I said.

'Holy Jeysus', said the diminutive one, 'Are ye not Matt Molloy?'

'Holy Jeysus I'm not', said I, delighted that someone would confuse me with a man who is possibly one of the finest flautists in all Ireland. Like me, Matt Molloy is balding and has a beard, and I suppose that through Guinness-soaked eyes one could be excused for noting a resemblance. The wee man was most apologetic, and insisted on showing me to the entire bar. 'Whad ye look at t'his fellas, is he not Matt Molloy's double?' For the first time in my life my balding head and beard earned me an entire evening of free Guinness. I now carry a flute in my top pocket... just in case history should repeat itself...

I was late in starting in the morning. I had a bit of a head and had some difficulty sorting out some of the recordings I had made the night before. It's amazing how material that

sounds great at one o'clock in the morning in a busy pub sounds awful in the cold grey light of dawn. Motoring over the Conair Pass to Cloghane, north of Dingle, I was dismayed to see Brandon cloaked in swirling mists and cloud. I had hoped for a view from the summit, a view which I'd been told the night before takes in the skyscrapers of New York!

Low cloud dominated the scene and I set off from the tiny village of Faha for what must be one of the most signposted mountain walks in the country. Signs proclaiming *Aire! Cnoc Gear* (Take care, Dangerous Hill) appear every couple of hundred yards. There is an annual pilgrimage walk to the summit of Brandon and the signposts are primarily for the benefit of pilgrims. Indeed at the start of the walk, just outside Faha, there is a grotto to the Blessed Virgin and I was delighted to see around it the first daffodils of the year. Spring at last. As confirmation of the fact, later in the day, I heard my first oystercatcher and curlew of the

Right *Warning signposts on the route up Brandon mark the pilgrims' trail to the summit* (Cameron McNeish).

Top right *Looking down the great 'coum' of Brandon, along the line of the Paternoster Lakes* (Cameron McNeish).

Bottom right *The author beside the remains of St Brendan's oratory on the summit of Brandon* (Cameron McNeish).

year. Good old Gulf Stream. Good old Ireland. Even in February she will bless you with her softness.

The path ran on into the murk of the mists. It was mild enough, but a real dampener. In several visits to Brandon I have only had it clear the once and I knew, as I surmounted the initial ridge and followed the path upwards, that I would soon be in one of the finest coums in Ireland. I longed to see it. Onwards I went, up steep slabs of rock, running with water. It's like climbing up a giant's staircase in this coum and on each giant-sized step there is a small tarn, still and black. These are the Paternoster Lakes; seen from above they resemble a Rosary chain! There was little in the

way of wildlife today. I've seen peregrines here, and buzzards, and fir club moss, starry saxifrage, wild thyme and St Patrick's Cabbage, the well-loved London Pride. But it was too early in the season for botany.

As I climbed up the last steep scree-filled section towards the summit ridge my miracle happened. A breeze, no doubt born somewhere beyond in the solitude of the wild Atlantic, caught the curtain of cloud and rent it apart, billowing it upwards, wrestling with it until it evaporated into streams far above me. The landscape that was revealed below made me gasp. Cliffs, broken and riven by great seams and clefts rose on all sides, the result of glaciation more than 12,000 years ago. The

loughs, each spilling over into another, dropped away like a string of black pearls as far as I could see into the peat-covered valley below. If there is such a thing as a Banshee, this must surely be its home. The whole place was glistening black and I loved it.

The summit ridge after this was something of an anticlimax, I longed to be back in the bowels of that deep natural gash. But duty bid and I duly made my pilgrimage to the ruins of St Brendan's oratory, right on the summit of this 3,127 ft mountain.

What a man St Brendan must have been. Instead of choosing a cave, or a forest, or even a lonely isle for his prayer cell, St Brendan chose the summit of this mountain, right on the very edge of the Atlantic. Perhaps it was the ensuing deprivations of fasting in such a wild spot that trained him for his later explorations. It is said that he made evangelical forays to France, England, Scotland and the Faroes. Indeed his *Navigatio*, a Latin account of journeys of Homeric proportions has enthralled generations and it was this journal that inspired an Englishman, Tim Severin, to undertake a voyage in Brendan's wake. This modern undertaking used a craft of Brendan's day, a leather-skinned curragh, to sail to Iceland and then America — a fabulous journey which proved that Brendan's original voyage, in the seventh century, was indeed possible.

It's now generally accepted that when Christopher Columbus landed in America, Vikings and Irish monks had preceded him.

> 'Do you remember Brandon,
> Our mountain in the west
> Brandon that looks on oceans
> Brandon of the Blessed?'

I wandered back down the ridge and into the depths of the coum, my mind full of great deeds. I was surprised to meet another walker.

'It's a grand day now,' I shouted.

'Indeed it is, Praise God,' was the reply, 'Yer man Brendan was a hardy one to be sure'. I agreed. Tom McDonagh was a schoolteacher from County Fermanagh, and he was on strike. He'd brought some school children down to Kerry for a few days but they in turn had gone on strike when they saw the weather that morning. We fell into easy conversation and found out that we had mutual friends in Dublin and in Glasgow.

Evening light on Mount Brandon, near to Dingle (Cameron McNeish).

We sat there talking and savouring our surroundings for a good hour, sharing our lunch and our mutual gossip. It was good to be there. The next day I had to drive north to County Clare in search of ancient music, which I didn't find. But it didn't matter. I had re-acquainted myself with the hills of Ireland, I had met friends, old and new, and I had even found springtime in a month that can be as wintry as any. Ireland had been good to me, yet again.

Three days after our meeting Tom

McDonagh was killed in a car accident. I read about his death in a Galway newspaper and I felt fortunate to have shared those moments with him on Brandon, his last mountain. However we come and go within this world, our existence is frail against the aeons of the hills. I am left with a February memory of a place and a time, edged with sadness for a friend I will not meet again on Brandon: Brendan's—and Tom's—hill.

Climbing, hill walking and folk music are the chief interests of Cameron McNeish who was born, and still lives in Scotland. The Editor of *Climber* magazine, Cameron has written seven books on outdoor subjects, including the *Backpacker's Manual, Backpacker's Scotland,* and *Ski The Nordic Way.* A regular broadcaster with the BBC in Scotland, Cameron McNeish also writes regularly for the Scottish press on outdoors matters.

March memories from the fireside

RICHARD GILBERT

When I sit dreaming beside the fire on long winter evenings my thoughts usually turn to past days in the hills. Such is the joy and intensity of pleasure that hill walking can bring to us, that experiences become indelibly ingrained on our minds, and memorable mountain days can be tucked away to be relived again and again. A typical and oft-recurring scene is set in the Western Highlands where, after a long and bitter winter, a high pressure system has become established and we steal a day on the Kintail ridges.

The month is March and the morning sun is just beginning to break through the early mist, the frost on the blades of grass is turning rapidly to dew and the mica schist crystals on

Sgurr na Ciste Duibhe — this is serious March 'hiking'! (Richard Gilbert).

the grey boulders are sparkling like diamonds. It has been a cold, crisp night: on the river thin plates of ice extend from the bank almost to mid-stream and, as we plod up the glen, the frozen puddles crunch and splinter under our boots.

By the time we have reached the 2,000 ft contour we have stripped down to shirtsleeves and are revelling in the warm rays of the sun, which is returning at last to northern latitudes. Spring is on the way and our spirits soar.

But once on the ridge the keen wind nips our ears and noses and we enter again a different world. The ferocity of the winter's storms is evident in the snow-plastered buttresses, the bottle green ice on the shallow lochan, blown clear by the gales sweeping over the bealach, and the massive cornices ringing the corries. Frost feathers stream from the rocks and snow devils whirl icy spicules into our eyes and down our necks.

Munching our sandwiches in the lee of a rock we have time to take stock and look around. White peaks thrust up into the blue sky at all points of the compass: from Ben Cruachan to An Teallach, and from the Cuillin of Skye to the Cairngorms, we renew acquaintance with the familiar forms of old friends. From our lofty perch we can look down to the glens, where estate workers are taking advantage of the dry spell to burn the heather, and a haze of blue smoke rolls up the hillside. A raven with glistening black feathers glides by, croaking a warning.

The days are lengthening and we can afford to amble over the snowy crests with equanimity, but eventually, with reluctance, we must turn down the steep spur to the glen. On the lower slopes the sun has softened the snow and rivulets of melt water are now running off the fast receding patches, turning the grass a livid green. The acrid smoke of the burning heather drifts up into our nostrils. By late afternoon we are back in the glen with the sun highlighting the brilliant white bark of the birch trees, while we rejoice at the drooping willows tinged with green, always the first sign of spring in the Highlands.

Idyllic March days stand out from the vagaries of our climate. Masefield's 'mad March days' are all too common in the hills, yet March brings hope of better things and I applaud the optimism of John Clare in his *Shepherd's Calendar* of 1827:

> 'March month of many weathers wildly comes
> In hail and snow and rain and threatening hums
> And floods: while often at his cottage door
> The Shepherd stands to hear the distant roar...
> Yet winter seems half weary of its toil
> And round the ploughman on the elting soil
> Will thread a minute's sunshine wild and warm
> Thro the raggd places of the swimming storm.'

For a varied and satisfying life we need contrast. Too much ease and indulgence at home make us hanker, eventually, for the primitive life of the mountains. Likewise remorseless sunshine, beating down day after day, parches the moorlands, cracks the peat,

Right *Near Sgurr na Ciste Duibhe on the Kintail ridges* (Richard Gilbert).

Below *Stac Polly from Beinn an Eoin — as impressive a view as any to be had on these cold bare slopes in March* (Richard Gilbert).

Below right *On Ben Alder, shadows are cast long by the early spring sun* (Richard Gilbert).

dries up the streams and saps our vitality. Before long we scan the horizon for storm clouds and welcome the fresh westerly wind bringing squalls of rain.

March provides extremes of climate and gives us the best of both worlds. Our northern hills retain dignity and stature under a mantle of winter snow; their broad ridges are plumed to sharp aretes, their plateaus are rippled and sculptured by drifts and their burns are alive with meltwater. The hills can still provide a stiff challenge to the mountaineer, for the unexpected is always lurking round the corner: perhaps a slope of steep windslab, a corniced arete or a verglassed rock buttress.

In early March 1963, after one of the most severe winters ever recorded (there was continuous frost from 22 December through to March), my wife and I camped on the spit of land between Buttermere and Crummock Water in the Lake District. The sun shone from a pale blue sky, the fells were hard as iron and no water flowed down the ice-choked rills and combes. Cars were driving across Derwent Water and Windermere, and we alternated between skating on Buttermere and walking the tops in some of the most arctic conditions ever seen in England. The thaw, when it came, was dramatic and sudden. When Kendal had its first rain for 74 days the River Kent was transformed within 24 hours from a dry bed to a deep and raging torrent, causing extensive flooding.

But March 1963 had another trick up its sleeve, with near dire consequences for us and our companions. Two weeks following the Kendal floods found us humping rucksacks into Knoydart, over the switchback path from Kinlochhourn. The sun blazed down, Loch Hourn shimmered a Mediterranean blue and primroses tentatively opened their buds on the sheltered banks of the burns. We climbed Ladhar Bheinn in warm sunshine, cooked supper over a driftwood fire and swam in Barrisdale Bay. The next day, still in shirtsleeves, we traversed Luinne Bheinn and Meall Buidhe and camped for the night high on the south-west ridge of Sgurr na Ciche. As the

sun set we could look straight down the full extent of Loch Nevis to the island of Eigg floating on a sea of gold: it was a magical moment and we thought nothing of the bank of grey clouds which rose in the west, or the first flap of the flysheet as a breeze got up.

Overnight the storm broke and winter returned with a bitter vengeance. Silver rain deposited a thin layer of ice on the rocks, while the wind threatened to pluck us off the ridge leading east over Garbh Chioch Mhor to Sgurr nan Coireachan; at times we were forced to crawl on hands and knees from rock to rock. Down in Glen Quoich the curtains of rain swept on ceaselessly, numbing our frozen bodies and transforming the tiniest trickle to a raging torrent. By now the saturated hillsides were white with water.

Our hearts sank still further when we met the Amhain Cosaidh burn: it roared across our path in a welter of foam, the top branches of trees just visible above the water, while beyond, tantalizingly, we could see the path continuing. Even with a safety rope the river was quite unfordable. Darkness fell as we struggled up the glen, trying unsuccessfully to cross the river at a higher point. Exhausted, we managed to erect a tent, placing huge boulders on the pegs. Nevertheless, the guy-ropes were snapping like cotton and, as we lay shuddering in our sodden sleeping bags, our once light-hearted expedition had become a nightmare.

On a happier note, by morning the gale had passed over leaving us limp and bruised, and highly respectful of the 'rough bounds' of Knoydart. We had learned the hard way that a carefree attitude to those balmy spring days of March must be tempered by caution. Snowdrops, primroses, aconites and the greening of buds in the sheltered glens can be misleading. Winter lingers long on the tops of our high mountains.

It is noticeable that the ptarmigan, that ubiquitous bird of the high mountain plateaus in Scotland, maintains its white winter plumage throughout most of the month of March. At that time of the year there is little life on the exposed boulder fields and I welcome the harsh warning croak of the ptarmigan and

attempt to pick him out against the background rocks.

If you are walking on the Cairngorm plateau in late March you might be lucky enough to see the flash of white wings from a flock of snow bunting. These little birds are probably en route to northern latitudes but a few pairs nest amongst the rocks, making them among the rarest of our breeding species. Mountain hares are widespread on the Scottish hills, and they too keep their white winter coats until well into March, when the first litters appear. Foxes cross the highest snowy ridges and although I have rarely seen them, I have often met their tracks, sometimes raised above the level of the snow where the wind has blown clear the unconsolidated powder on either side.

A severe winter can be devastating for the red deer population of the Highlands, and by March they are often weak and starving. Although the calves are born in the summer months, and the hind continues to suckle her calf until February, it has been estimated (F. Fraser-Darling) that about 40 per cent of calves perish during the first winter. New forestry plantations and the accompanying fencing has

Walking becomes scrambling and then climbing on Sgoran Dubh — preparation for the worst is the key to a good day out (Richard Gilbert).

March in Glen Callater is for those not over-awed by snow-splashed hills since frozen ground actually makes walking easier (Richard Gilbert).

denied large feeding areas to deer and this has exacerbated the problem. In early spring I have often seen deer struggling in soft, marshy ground, without the strength to run away. After the exceptionally cold winter of 1979 I walked through Glen Tilt, from Blair Atholl to the Bedford Memorial Bridge over the river Tarf, and passed no less than seven emaciated and very dead deer lying near the river. Edward Thomas is right when he writes, in his poem *March:*

> 'The sunset piled
> Mountains and mountains of snow and
> ice in the west:
> Somewhere among their folds the wind
> was lost,
> And yet, 'twas cold, and though I knew
> that Spring
> Would come again, I knew it had not
> come,
> That it was lost too in those mountains
> chill.'

Weather records show that it was on 6 March 1967 that an anemometer, on a pylon supporting the Coire Cas chairlift on Cairn Gorm, recorded a gust of 125 knots, to establish a record wind speed for mainland Britain. Likewise, measurements of the depth of snow on the summit plateau of Ben Nevis, indicate that the seasonal maximum depth is not attained until 15 April as an average date.

Snow and high winds must be expected in March, and hill walking becomes much more exciting, challenging and exhilarating because of this. March is an emotive month for me and the word alone triggers the happiest of memories. How can I ever forget the 1,500 ft continuous standing glissade, from the summit of Carn Mor Dearg to the CIC hut under the north face of Ben Nevis, the waist deep powder snow in Glen Bianasdail as we fought our way up Slioch, or the bite of our crampons as we traversed the icy slopes above the giant cornices overhanging the Garbh Choire of Braeriach? Then there was the day on the

South Kintail ridge, when we were confronted by 50 ft plumes of snow, blown up by gale force winds from the corrie below Aonach Air Chrith.

Yet, such is the unpredictable nature of the British climate, that I have known years when the An Teallach traverse has been virtually free of snow by late March, and we have swum in Loch Coire Mhic Fhearchair on Beinn Eighe. In such years you can look out in March for the Purple Mountain Saxifrage (*Saxifraga oppositifolia*), coming into bloom in sheltered gullies, cracks and buttresses, particularly on slightly alkaline terrain such as Ben Lawers and Helvellyn. Purple Mountain Saxifrage is the earliest of our mountain flowers and its southern limit in England is the Pennine hills of Ingleborough and Pen-y-ghent, where it flourishes on the north facing cliffs of Yoredale limestone at a height of 2,000 ft. It has occupied these same ledges since the end of the last great ice age, some 10,000 years or so ago.

March is the best month for winter climbing. The snow in the gullies has consolidated and the days are long enough for some of the classic snow and ice routes of the Highlands to be attempted. To emerge into bright sunshine on the summit plateau or Ben Nevis, Lochnagar or Beinn Laoigh, having struggled in the icy shadows on such routes as Gardyloo, Raeburn's or Central Gully, is to experience a unique feeling of joy and satisfaction that is unknown to ordinary mortals. The constrictions of the climb, the claustrophobia, the taut muscles and the pumping adrenalin are suddenly replaced by expansive views, dazzling snow fields, space where you can ease and stretch your limbs, and a release of nervous energy amounting to ecstasy.

The buttresses and ridges on the north face of Ben Nevis provide the longest climbs (up to 2,000 ft) in the British Isles and, on sunny days in March, they can offer truly Alpine experiences. Tower Ridge, Observatory Ridge and North East Buttress are the principal natural features on the face and, since their exploration at the turn of the century, have justifiably earned classic status. Highlights which I shall never forget are edging across the razor sharp arete of Tower Gap between plunging gullies of grey ice, kicking up the

Left *The summit of Marsco proud against the skyline on a cold clear March day* (Richard Gilbert).

Below left *The approach to Beinn Dearg Mor* (Richard Gilbert).

néve on the upper reaches of Observatory Ridge in complete freedom, while the sound of other climbers chipping hard ice drifted up from Zero and Point Five gullies on either side, and pulling over the ten foot vertical step of ice, known as the Man Trap, near the top of North East buttress with a grin of satisfaction, knowing that the last problem on the route had been cracked and the summit plateau was near at hand.

If March is welcomed by the hill walker and the snow and ice climber it is no less awaited by the backpacker. The backpacker can get to know the mountains in their every mood. The remotest folds, glens and corries can be explored at leisure for there are no deadlines, no schedules and no fixed routes. The backpacker is a self-contained unit with tent, equipment, stove and provisions and he or she can wander at will, and camp rough at any suitable site and at any time.

In modern life we are herded here, there and everywhere. We live strictly controlled lives. Forms must be filled in, bills paid, cars driven, queues joined and alarm clocks set for the morning. But the backpacker can forget the external pressures of the twentieth century and escape to freedom. He can sit back and reflect objectively on life, he can re-adjust his priorities and he has the chance to make decisions for the future. A few days completely away from civilization, camping high in the mountains, is guaranteed to refresh the mind, relax the body and improve one's sanity.

Nowadays, equipment is so good that the backpacker can enjoy life in remote mountain ranges, secure and confident that his tent is stormproof and his sleeping bag warm. When you have been battling all day against the elements you need proper protection from them at night.

Perhaps the key to enjoyable backpacking is the weight of the rucksack, for if it is too heavy it will sap your energy and drain your vitality. Far too many walkers struggle over the hills, bent double with huge packs and, with sweat pouring into their eyes, they are unable to appreciate their surroundings. The day's outing has become a drudge. March is an ideal month for backpacking. You don't get too hot under the weight of your rucksack, you have the choice of camping above or below the snow-line and there are no midges.

In the early days, when my life-long love of

Looking west from Ben More Coigach—an archipelago lonely and remote hovers between sea and stormy sky (Richard Gilbert).

the Highlands of Scotland was beginning to blossom, I was fascinated by the huge tract of mountainous country encompassing the three great glens of the Western Highlands: Glens Affric, Cannich and Strathfarrar. It was obvious that a backpacking expedition would be necessary to reach the innermost sanctuaries of the mountains. My friend Alan shared my enthusiasm for the Highlands and we planned a route around the ridges overlooking Loch Mullardoch in Glen Cannich.

We set off in mid-March. It was bitterly cold and we toiled over the snow-covered ridges of Sgurr na Lapaich and An Riabhachan, sometimes wearing crampons and sometimes cutting steps. Although the weather was mainly poor with mist and snow flurries, the occasional gap in the clouds showed the surrounding peaks as white giants against a blue sky. From Mam Sodhail shafts of sunlight played on the surface of Loch Affric far below, and the sight of the old pine forest at the edge of the loch made a welcome change from our white world. Arctic hares, ptarmigan and snow bunting abounded, and a dark brown fox emerged from the boulders at the summit of

Sgurr nan Ceathreamhnan. At nightfall we erected the tent on the nearest flat platform we could find, settled down in our sleeping bags and cooked by candlelight. Our boots froze solid at night and the eggs had to be prized out of their shells, but all was forgotten in the evening when we lay smoking our pipes, sipping whisky and calculating the day's tally of Munros.

On the fifth day, as we approached the summit of our last peak, Toll Creagach, the clouds rolled away and bathed the ridges and glens in warm sunshine. Bursting with fitness and high spirits we romped down the snow fields to the heather and scrub birch in Glen Cannich. It had been an experience of a lifetime, and had introduced us to the possibilities of rewarding adventure that await the hill walker in early spring. We were hooked, and from that day onwards the month of March and the Scottish hills became synonymous.

We are extremely fortunate in Britain in possessing a magnificently wild and rugged coastline. There is a close affinity between a cliff-girt coastline and a mountain face: rock

The staunch headlands of carboniferous limestone near Mewslade Bay, Gower (Richard Gilbert).

climbers gain particular pleasure from sea-cliff climbing, hill walkers derive satisfaction from following a switchback route along a rocky coast and many mountain lovers have turned to the sea for recreation in later life. The sea's constant ebb and flow, accompanied by the roar and suck of the breakers, is akin to the buffeting and moaning of the wind, and the slow erosion of our mountain peaks by frost and rain. In both cases we can closely observe the forces of nature at work.

I enjoy nothing more than a bracing walk along an exposed coastline, when March gales are driving Atlantic rollers against a splintered shore. In March the kiosks and ice-cream parlours are still battened down for the winter, sandy bays are unmarked by footprints and, apart from the screaming gulls, you have the cliff-tops to yourself. For those walkers who are impatient to forget the winter and welcome the spring, March in Cornwall or along the south-west coast of Britain will not disappoint them. Daffodils are flowering in the sheltered vales and gorse blooms on the edge of the cliffs.

Shakespeare writes in *The Winter's Tale:*

'... daffodils,
That come before the swallow dares, and take
The winds of March with beauty; violets dim,
But sweeter than the lids of Juno's eyes
Or Cytherea's breath; pale prime-roses
That die unmarried, ere they can behold
Bright Phoebus in his strength.'

Walk from Lamorna Cove to Land's End and scramble up the rough boulders to Logan Rock, explore the deserted open-air theatre at Porth Curno, marvel at the waves creaming over the Runnel Stone and peer over the steepling granite cliffs of Chair Ladder at Tol-Pedn-Penwith. The sunlight sparkles off the sea and the wind brings tears to the eyes, but the air is a tonic and soon dispels the gloom of the long winter months.

North, across the Bristol Channel, we have a change of scene. The underlying bedrock of carboniferous limestone has been buckled and folded, producing the dramatic scenery of the Gower Peninsula. West from the Mumbles stretches a wild and rugged coastline of white limestone cliffs, headlands, reefs, coves, inlets, caves, blow-holes and wide sandy bays. When I walked this coast in early March a stiff breeze was whipping the tops of the waves into white horses, and lines of surf were streaming across the firm sands of Brandy Cove, Langland Bay and Caswell Bay.

From Pwlldu Head, at just over 300 ft, I could barely make out the grey outline of the north Devon coast across the Bristol Channel, but my attention was focused on the vast sweep of Oxwich Bay, two miles to the west. I approached the bay with a thrill of anticipation for the sunshine was glistening on the wet sand and prows of white limestone ran out boldly towards the breaking waves. The tide was fully out and I ran with sheer exuberance across Threecliff Bay. Rock climbers provided a splash of colour on the clean buttresses and I was able to squeeze round the seaward end of Great Tor which divides Threecliff Bay from the main curve of Oxwich Bay.

For an hour I walked along the sand in complete solitude, save for a few oyster-catchers turning over the scallops and razor shells with their red beaks. In contrast to the wide sands of the bay, the slopes of Oxwich Point are wooded with oak, ash, elm, hazel and hawthorn. Many of the trees were in bud and birds were twittering in the branches: a carpet of snowdrops surrounded the tiny 13th century church of St Illtyd's, set just above high water mark. This magnificent walk continues along the romantic and historic Gower Coast to Worms Head, traversing cliff tops of springy turf with the surging sea constantly pounding the rocks below.

For sheer desolation and majesty of scenery, however, we must travel to the furthest extremity of Britain, to the far-flung headland of Cape Wrath in Sutherland. The nearest public road is ten miles from the Cape, although a private minibus service links the ferry at Kyle of Durness to the lighthouse.

Stand beside the lighthouse above the 400 ft cliffs of grey Lewisian gneiss, and feel the ground tremble as the combers crash against the oldest rock in Britain. There are few signs of spring up here in the far north in March and the gales are frequent. Storms out in the North Atlantic send huge seas rolling eastwards to the Scottish mainland. With a clap of thunder the waves spend their energy on the base of the cliffs, sending columns of spray hundreds of feet into the air.

In spite of this demoniacal scene the fulmars and kittiwakes glide effortlessly around the cliffs and stacks, while rafts of guillemots and razorbills ride the swell beyond the breakers. With luck you might see an early puffin.

If you turn your head south you can see the long line of surf at Sandwood Bay, the off-shore islets of Am Balg and the rock pinnacle of Am Buachaille. The walk south to Sandwood Bay and beyond to the crofting village of Sheigra gives a rough trek of twelve miles. Headlands, moors, gullies, inlets, bays and streams must be negotiated and there is no path. On a bright March day, the white-capped peaks of Beinn Spionnaidh, Cranstackie and Foinaven glint in the sunshine away to the east, complementing the lumpy green sea, boiling white against the cliffs.

The adventurous walker cannot fail to be enthralled by Sandwood Bay. A mile of firm sand is bounded by the open Atlantic on one side whence the waves thunder on the shores.

On the other side sand-dunes and marram grass hold back a lagoon, and grassy slopes lead up to a haunted cottage which overlooks a lonely loch. The surrounding cliffs, the watchful 200 ft high pinnacle of rock, the turbulent sea and the emptiness give one a feeling of awe and reverence unique to Britain.

In our search for rugged sea-swept coastlines we must visit Orkney, perhaps the most exquisite jewel of all. The Mainland, Orkney's largest island, is flat and cultivated, but the western coast from the Brough of Birsay to Stromness is exposed to the elements and gives us another exhilarating walk of twenty miles through majestic scenery.

The adventure begins as soon as you embark on the steamer at Scrabster for, in March, the Pentland Firth is likely to be rough. On my last visit I hauled myself on deck, with heaving stomach, to admire the 450 ft Old Man of Hoy, and the gigantic cliffs of St John's Head, at 1,100 ft the highest in the British Isles, excluding St Kilda.

The following morning I set off south from Brough of Birsay in bright winter sunshine and in high spirits. The scene was a kaleidoscope

Birsay bay, Orkney has all the features which epitomize these northern shores (Richard Gilbert).

The Old Man of Hoy, Orkney is a well-known challenge to climbers and a dramatic sight for the walker (Richard Gilbert).

of colour: a restless blue sea with white horses, creamy surf, red sandstone cliffs capped with green turf, and a huge expanse of azure sky above. The walk south passes the Kitchener Memorial tower on Marwick Head, and the prehistoric stone-age village of Skara Brae but, as usual, it was the natural features that impressed me most of all. The entire seventeen-mile coastline is made up of towering cliffs, inlets, geos, stacks and natural arches and, as with the Sutherland coast, it was quite deserted. The cliff tops were littered with slivers of rock and flat stones, whirled up from below and indicative of the fury of the winter storms in this remote region. It is a bracing experience to walk over these dizzying heights.

Nearer to home however, my favourite and more usual weekend stamping grounds are the Northern Pennines and the Scottish Borders. These remote and desolate fells are at their best in March when old snow drifts are still banked up under the hedges and dry-stone walls, the arctic wind ruffles the wool of the timid Swaledale ewes, and the pools and peat hags are still frozen and firm.

In summer the bleak hills of Teesdale, Weardale, Kielder, the Cheviots and Galloway are tough going: the deep coarse grass and heather tug at your boots like barbed wire, and you must fight your way through the waist-high bracken which clothes the valley sides. But return to the fells in March, when the tussocks have been flattened by the winter snows and rains and the bracken is withered and matted, then you can stride unfettered through the upland valleys and along the broad ridges. After a frosty night you can crunch across the normally hideous black bogs and peat hags of Bleaklow and, in Northumberland, you may even be able to reach the summit trig point on Cheviot, usually a titanic struggle through a knee-deep quagmire.

High on many of the fells, springs gush to the surface from far underground, and the thread-like streams foam down the hillsides, cutting deep gullies through to the bedrock. In places strata of hard rocks cause cataracts and falls and, in severe March gales, the water is

Liathach looking to Flowerdale — is it any wonder that such a scene should remain fixed in one's memory? (Richard Gilbert).

blown straight back up the hill in a cloud of spray.

Cross Fell, High Cup Nick, Mickle Fell, Rogan's Seat, Killhope Law, Burnhope Seat and Peel Fell will provide wonderful challenges in March: long days on wild, windswept and remote fells, with solid, stone-built farmhouses nestling in the valleys, and perhaps a few ancient mine workings and spoil heaps on the tops as a reminder of the industrial activity of previous centuries.

At the end of the day, when the sun sets and the temperature drops, there will be warm hospitality and blazing log fires in the village inns. Put up your feet, order your pint and reflect on the diverse pleasures of the day: perhaps you have savoured the hills for the last time in winter and can look ahead to the spring, for March bridges the seasons and can truly give you the best of both.

Richard Gilbert was born in Lancaster in 1937. He read chemistry at Oxford where he was President of the University Mountaineering Club. After working in industry he became a teacher at Ampleforth College near York. He completed the Munros (the 3,000 ft peaks of Scotland) in 1971 and in 1977 won a Winston Churchill Fellowship for leading the first ever schools expedition to the Himalayas. His books include the best sellers *Big Walks* and *Classic Walks*.

High April moors and deep Derbyshire dales

PETER CLOWES

The rain-spattered winds that speed across the Cheshire Plain and howl around the jumbled rocks of Kinder Scout in April seem sharper and fresher than any that have battered the barren hillsides in winter. I usually set out on my first walk of the year over the high country of the Derbyshire Peak District just before Easter. The annual crop of orange peel, lager cans and plastic bags has not yet bloomed around the lofty Downfall at holiday weekends. I sit at peace on a smooth boulder and look down at the rugged brown landscape below my outstretched boots.

The infant River Kinder, here only a few feet wide, meanders sluggishly through a maze of peaty hollows that cover the 2,000 ft Scout and topples off the plateau at the Downfall over a stairway of gritstone slabs. Several hundred feet below, perhaps half a mile away in a fold of the moor, the green water of tiny Mermaid Pool lies half-hidden behind a screen of yellow reeds. Farther down the valley is Kinder Reservoir, its inlets and bays spreading out like the legs of a great grey spider.

If you are lucky enough to be on Kinder on a blustery April day after a night of rain you can catch the Downfall in effervescent mood. The spray from its 100 ft high stream of white water is flung impressively skywards in a feathery misty plume. It is a remarkable sight

Peakland panorama: Chinley Churn and Gritstone sheep (Peter Clowes).

— one that can sometimes be seen from the streets of Stockport twelve miles away. 'The old woman is brewing', the villagers of Hayfield used to say.

The best walk over Kinder starts from a small car park in a disused quarry near Hayfield. In April rabbits hop between car and caravan wheels and jackdaws cackle around their nests on a towering rock wall that faces the river. A footpath crosses the slender stone arch of Bowden Bridge and climbs to Hill Houses Farm, where a convenient wide road hewn out of the slope for tractors follows the valley contours to Farlands Booth. Across the lane there is a narrow wooden gate and a footpath under the trees along the left bank of the River Kinder. A steep rocky path leads up the side of the high grassy bank of Kinder Dam and, immediately, there are soul-stirring, pulse-racing views of the escarpment ahead. The steep face is littered with dark boulders, through which plunges the shadowy cleft of Red Brook like a dagger slash in a huge brown cushion.

It was from this airy viewpoint that Mrs Humphrey Ward, a popular Victorian writer, described Kinder in her novel *The History of David Grieve*. When the book's hero, young David Grieve, ran along the banks of the River Kinder on a clear April morning the valley had not yet been dammed.

'Beyond the undulating heather ground at his feet', wrote Mrs Ward, 'rose a magnificent curving front of moor, the steep sides of it crowned with black edges and cliffs of grit, the outline of the south-western end sweeping finely up on the right to a purple peak, the king of all the moorland round.'

The path climbs steeply up William Clough. A heather-covered slope leading up to Leygatehead Moor fills most of the western sky. A stream tumbles down an uneven flight of rocky steps. The only sounds are the plops and gurgles of the water, a hiss of wind over the tufty grass and faint calls from newly-born lambs in the fields below. Each step up the zig-zag path makes the heart pump. Cock wheatears bob their white rumps on the

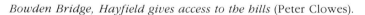

Bowden Bridge, Hayfield gives access to the hills (Peter Clowes).

Above *Mount Famine and South Head as they appear from the Kinder valley* (Peter Clowes).

Right *This signpost on Middle Moor near William Clough never fails to offer advice!* (Peter Clowes).

stubbly rocks a few yards ahead and tawny little meadow pipits flutter over thick clumps of spiky grass that lean over the limpid water.

There has been a path up William Clough, over the side of Kinder and down into Woodlands Valley for centuries. When the then Duke of Devonshire closed it in 1876 — it interfered with his grouse shooting — a long and vigorous campaign was waged to reopen the route. Twenty years later the battle was won and a procession, led by a brass band, marched through the village of Hayfield to celebrate.

But it was on the moor above William Clough on a crisp April day in 1932 that the famous 'mass trespass', sometimes called the Battle of Kinder Scout, occurred. After many years of futile negotiations with grouse-shooting landowners, principally the Manchester warehouse tycoon James Watts, members of the British Workers' Sports Federation organized a gathering of 500 young

Rocks on the Kinder escarpment (Peter Clowes).

ramblers on Hayfield recreation ground on the morning of Sunday 24 April. They marched up the lane to Kinder Reservoir and along the path to William Clough. Then, on a blast from a whistle, they turned right and struck directly up the moor towards the crest of Kinder.

A party of gamekeepers armed with sticks barred their path. There was a lot of shouting and a certain amount of pushing before the marchers swept on up the slope and on to Ashop Head, where they met a small group of fellow-demonstrators who had walked from Edale. The ramblers sang the Red Flag (the BWSF had strong left-wing leanings) and marched back down the valley into Hayfield. Police were awaiting them. Four men were arrested and charged with riotous assembly, trespass and assault. All but one were eventually found guilty and given prison sentences of up to six months.

The marchers' boisterous demonstration against the 19th century Enclosure Acts, however, gave considerable impetus to the long and more orderly campaign conducted by the Ramblers' Federation, the Peak District and Northern Counties Footpath Preservation Society and other bodies to gain access to large areas of privately-owned countryside. In 1951 Parliament designated the Peak District as Britain's first national park — and Kinder Scout

was open to everyone. One can almost hear the ghostly cries of battling ramblers and gamekeepers below the shoulder of Sandy Heys as the last few hundred yards of William Clough are surmounted.

On Ashop Head, a wind-swept saddle separating Kinder from Mill Hill to the west, there is a well-trodden track joining the William Clough path at right angles. It comes down from Kinder, skirting boulders, zig-zagging through the peat hags. This is the Pennine Way, which starts five miles away in Edale village, turns north on Mill Hill and runs for 200 miles to the Scottish border. I like to sit on a rock at the top of William Clough and look down the valley, listening to the wind and watching the clouds glide over Chinley Churn like an armada sweeping across the landscape with well-filled sails.

The top of Kinder Scout, 2,000 ft high and marked 'The Peak' on many maps, is anything but dramatic. It is a flat wasteland of deeply-fissured black peat with outcrops of rock on its edges that have been weathered by wind and rain into weird shapes. It is the nearest thing to wilderness that we have in England — and that

is why I adore it.

On a week-day in April you meet very few walkers trudging along the Pennine Way. Red grouse — one of the few bird species indigenous to Britain — fly low over the moor. Sometimes an early long-legged curlew, a large grey bird with a long curved bill, can be seen strutting along the crests of deep 'groughs'. And there are, invariably, a number of Derbyshire Gritstone sheep grazing amid the rocks, bilberry and fresh heather. The Kinder plateau, together with a couple of adjoining farms, was purchased by the National Trust in 1982 for £600,000 and sheep grazing is now strictly controlled to allow the natural vegetation to recover and, hopefully, flourish.

The Downfall is soon reached from Ashop Head. Streaks of snow on the flat rocks flanking the narrow gorge present a vivid backdrop to Kinder's corrugated escarpment. When April blizzards sweep across the Peak the whole Downfall is turned into an

The infant River Kinder at the top of the Downfall (Peter Clowes).

one thing that is indisputable: no-one walks over the Kinder plateau without visiting the Downfall at some time or other. On summer weekends walkers who sometimes gather in large groups on rocks on either side can give the area an appearance of a bizarre market-place.

There is a choice of routes along the western edge of the escarpment. Three clearly-marked paths wind through rocks lying amid turf and heather immediately below the dark desert of the plateau. I prefer to stride out along the highest path, following the stony trail that picks its way through a maze of sticky, boot-clinging peat. There are small pools of coffee-coloured water gleaming in hollows beneath the rippled crests of this wind-swept petrified ocean. Only after some time does a lone trig column, perched on a cluster of grey boulders in a patch of flinty shingle, come into view. This is the second-highest point on the Scout, 2,077 ft above sea level. The main trig point, a mere 11 ft higher, lies nearly a mile away to the north-east over the boggy channels. This is one of the flattest hill-tops in Britain.

The long shoulder of Brown Knoll and the peak of its adjoining satellite, South Head, confront the walker as he nears the end of Kinder and passes an outcrop of fragmented rock known as the Swine's Back. It is pleasant, high-level walking country here through clumps of thick heather and cotton grass. On the saddle between Kinder and Brown Knoll, overlooking a bowl in the hills where the River Sett is born, stands Edale Cross. This old stone pillar, a boundary mark at the centre of the ancient Royal Forest of the Peak, was found lying on the ground in 1810 by local farmer John Gee. He and his neighbours re-erected it, carving the year and their initials on its side. Past the cross runs a broad sandy track along which teams of packhorses would plod until the railways put them out of business. This was one of the main routes through the Pennines from the towns of Cheshire and Lancashire to the growing cities of Yorkshire.

I climbed up this path from Hayfield one April day when a teeth-chattering wind that was howling over the moor had filled every crevice of the broken walls with thin ribbons

enormous icefall, with icicles hanging from the slabs to sparkle in the watery sunshine like great silver organ pipes.

Walkers have mixed opinions about the Downfall. 'An untidy mess', writes Wainwright, who nevertheless goes on to admit that the scenery from the head of the fall is 'spectacular'. A 'monumental and profound ravine', says Mark Richards in his guide book. Others have described the fall as 'impressive' but 'disappointing in dry weather'. There is

Right *Map of Kinder Scout walk.*

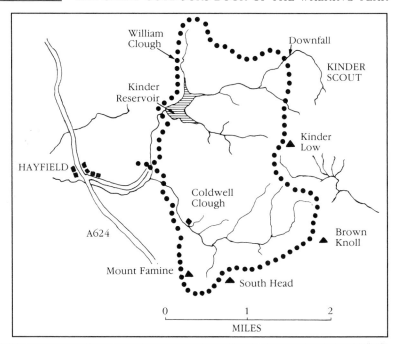

Below *The high plateau of Kinder Scout (Peter Clowes).*

of snow. There was half-an-inch of grey, squelchy slush under my boots as I crossed the saddle and thought about the packhorse 'jaggers' who came this way in the 18th century with their strings of German ponies — sometimes as many as fifty animals, each carrying two panniers loaded with coal or salt.

The horses had bells attached to their harness and their approach could be heard from miles away. I thought of the old inns in the Peakland valleys where the 'jaggers' spent the night and their animals were tethered with a guard on their unhitched panniers. To this day there is a Scotsman's Pack Inn at Hathersage, a Packhorse Inn at Chapel-en-le-Frith and a 15th century Packhorse in Hayfield village.

Where the path drops towards the Edale valley, down an abrupt slope known as Jacob's Ladder, I leaned on a weathered stone gatepost and looked across a great curve of snow-flecked grass that forms the south-eastern face of Kinder. On the skyline above were the layered slabs of Noe Stool and, at the far end, the blunt, battleship-prow pinnacle of Crowden Tower.

I turned south, away from the packhorse trail, and followed a faint path, little clearer than a sheep-track, that climbed towards Brown Knoll, the 1,866 ft highest point of the Colborne ridge. Here is one of England's slenderest watersheds. Damp turf on the western side of the ridge indicates the birth of the infant River Sett that eventually flows into

the Goyt, the Mersey and the Irish Sea. On my left lay several dark, brackish pools marking the start of a tributary of the River Noe that flows to the North Sea via the Trent and Humber.

There was no sign of the colourful crested plovers that would be seen wheeling over the moor in a few weeks' time. Only an occasional carrion crow, its wings ragged in the wind, was being swept across the sky like a bundle of black rags. At Dimpus Gate, where the high country dips between Brown Knoll and 1,600 ft South Head, I sheltered behind a draughty stone wall and looked down on Dimpus Clough where the tiny River Sett was glinting through spidery copses of bare trees. 'It is, indeed, the finest Alpine picture to be obtained in the whole Peak District', wrote Tallent Bateman, who walked here ninety years ago. I find it difficult to disagree with him.

Faint haze hung over the houses of Hayfield in the distance. Ragged threads of blue smoke rose from the tiny buildings of Coldwell Clough and South Head Farms, which perched on the bare hillside like children's bricks on a worn brown carpet. Swine's Back jutted into the dark-grey clouds massed over Kinder, but the sky was brightening in the west. The snow had stopped and a small, hardly-perceptible patch of sunlight was creeping stealthily towards me over the ragged walls and pale green pastures of the Sett valley.

The days when workmen chopped down alder trees growing on the banks of the Sett have long gone. In the 18th century they would wait for the winter floods, saw the trees into short lengths and send logs plunging down the stream to Hayfield. There the water-resistant wood was manufactured into clogs, butter boards and burned into charcoal to make gunpowder.

As I walked on, along a wide, terraced track that crossed the slope of South Head, a flag-roofed barn and two other outbuildings appeared in the shelter of a clump of dark trees far below. This was Coldwell Clough Farm, where I once used to call for a farmhouse tea after the long tramp over Jacob's Ladder from Edale. The property has not been lived in for some years, but members of the Bradbury family farmed there from the 14th century until about 1940. In one stone building is a double-seated lavatory, in another a salting stone where pigs were once killed and rubbed with salt, and on the gable end of the big barn perches a stone monkey.

A chestnut-coloured kestrel hovered over the moor, its wings fluttering rapidly, its tail spread like a fan, and I remembered the condition under which King Edward the First originally gave the land that surrounds Coldwell Clough Farm to his constable, Edmund Bradbury: 'A head of game will be preserved for falconry for the king and his men.' Happily, the farm, with

Far left *Dimpus Gate below South Head — with Mount Famine beyond* (Peter Clowes).

Left *The Mount Famine path with South Head to the right* (Peter Clowes).

Below *Swine's Back, Kinder Scout, stands out against the sky when viewed from the Mount Famine path* (Peter Clowes).

its small mullioned windows and cobbled yard, is now a protected building.

My path crossed a short saddle linking South Head with Mount Famine (1,450 ft) and I glanced over a drunken wall topped with rusty wire on my left. A slope ran down towards several small farms. About three miles off stood the conical peak of Eccles Pike, with the boat-shaped plateau of Combs Moss just protruding around the western shoulder of South Head. Long streaks of pearl-grey cloud lined the pale sky and the wiry grass around my feet skipped and danced as a fresh breeze swept across the bare brown flank of Mount Famine.

Oblivious to the wind, several sheep grazed placidly on the hill. Hundreds of hardy Derbyshire Gritstones roam these moors — and it's big business. When Kinder Scout was for sale a few years ago a local sheep farmer paid £40,000 for grazing rights alone. The Gritstones, which are hornless and have distinctive black and white faces and legs, are an ancient breed. 'On their native heath, amidst ling and furze, rocks and boulders, they are exceptionally hardy and wiry,' said the Breeders' Society when it was formed in 1907. Their wool is tight and dense and well adapted to withstand heavy Pennine storms.

Later in the year more sheep would be on the hills where I walked. Many ewes were now with new-born lambs in the barns and paddocks in the valleys — the sound of their bleating, and the excited barking of sheepdogs, drifted up to me from the Andrews Farm which lay about half a mile down the slope.

I now climbed over the western flank of Mount Famine and, turning my back on the dark crest of Chinley Churn, pushed open a rust-festooned iron gate that was hinged on its stump by loops of coarse plastic string, squeezed past several black heifers stamping the ground around the gate into a quagmire and followed a track that slanted down the hillside towards the River Sett. Soon I was on a firm lane, part of the old trail to Coldwell Clough and Edale. Along here in 1736 travelled James Clegg, a clergyman and farmer from Chinley who was also the Peak District doctor.

'I rode over into Kinder to see widow Bradbury's children,' he wrote in April that year. 'They are ill of the smallpox. I prayed with them and returned at night much fatigued.' A later entry in his diary records a visit to Coldwell Clough to baptise 'a weakly child'. He dined at the farm and had 'a

hazardous journey' back to his home at Stodhart. When storms raged over the High Peak in those days the doctor needed a special kind of courage to leave his cosy fireside and ride for miles to visit his sick patients.

The lane brought me back to my starting point at Bowden Bridge and the River Kinder. As I groped in the bottom of my rucksack for the last chocolate bar of the day, two white-bibbed dippers flew downstream over the rushing water. Inside a barn at the farm nearby more sheep were bleating their impatience for the hills. Rabbits were still frolicking in the car park, while over the trees a small circle of blue sky bore promise of other times to come. An April day on Kinder takes a lot of beating.

But the charm of the Peak is not confined to the high gritstone moors. The deep dales of the softer limestone country are of completely different character and can satisfy the most demanding walker. Particularly in April. One chilly but clear spring morning I hoisted my rucksack over my shoulders and set off along the smooth, wide track of finely-crushed limestone that runs alongside the River Wye not far from Buxton.

Sunshine had not yet penetrated the dale and there was heavy dew on the grass. Topley Pike, a prominent pinnacle of crinkly limestone, frowned down from beyond the main Buxton to Bakewell road. The milky-green river flowed sluggishly at my side between banks shrouded in musty-smelling dock leaves rocking gently in the breeze on tall rhubarb-like stems. Small trout occasionally dimpled the surface of the stream. It must, I thought, be very frustrating for the angler. This was not a good stretch for the casting of fine nylon lines — the river bank was overgrown and laced with stringy weeds.

The path went through woods covering both sides of the river and twice passed under high stone-and-brick piers of railway viaducts, the tops of which seemed to be enveloped in the leafless canopies of the trees. At the side of a third viaduct a flight of steps, dug out of the slope and packed with limestone chippings behind stoutly-pegged logs of pine, brought me up to the disused track of the old Midland railway line that once ran through the Wye gorge.

This was the start of the Monsal Trail, a popular walking route that meanders for eight miles through Chee Dale, Millers Dale and Monsal Dale and includes two short tunnels. The views from the old trackbed, now cindered and partly overgrown but in some places still rough with limestone ballast, are quite spectacular. Great canyon walls of rock tower on either side. The river below glints and winks as it bubbles madly over submerged boulders and glides swiftly between banks of dock and water lily.

From the edge of the viaduct I looked down on to a row of blue-slated houses known as Blackwell Cottages, where the valley is joined by Great Rocks Dale, a narrow fissure that has suffered much depredation at the explosive hands of quarry owners for more than a century. Chee Dale is at its widest point here, the northern side swelling in a lofty green slope up to Old Moor with crags shooting through the turf and the grassy ridge streaked here and there with gorse and scrub and an occasional patch of dark trees. A wooden footbridge crossed the Wye and a riverside path, knee-deep in ferns, vanished into a small forest of thorns and alders that obscured the sinuous river.

I headed along the trail through the arch of a stone bridge and under the prominent brow of Plum Buttress, a wall of firm grey limestone on which several red-helmeted climbers were clinging like beetles, their nylon ropes draped across the rock face in great loops of green and blue. The dark half-moon portal of a tunnel, partly screened by mountain ash and silver birch, lay in my path. Daylight could be seen about 200 yards ahead but it was an eerie sensation to hear my boots crunching the gravel as I walked under the echoing smoke-blackened brickwork. There were little 'sentry-box' shelters in the curved sides where platelayers once stood with glowing lamps as Pullman expresses thundered through on their way to St Pancras.

Out in the open valley again the track ran along a terrace, a smooth vertical rock wall on my left, a steep, grassy, shrub-covered slope down to the river on my right. Somewhere below a pheasant called. The rough grass was speckled with the petals of bright yellow vetch and tall-stemmed ragwort. High ferns fringed the river. The writer R. Murray Gilchrist once said that to see Chee Dale to perfection one

Map of Monsal Trail walk.

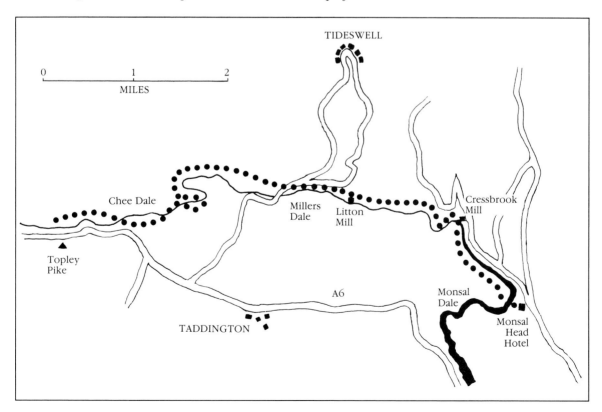

A school party waits to walk along the stepping stones in Chee Dale (Peter Clowes).

Above April: *The bulk of Kinder Scout rises sullenly, even on a bright day, above the reservoir with its grassy dam* (Peter Clowes).

Below April: *Typical of the often difficult going on top of Kinder is this peat bog. In the centre background can be seen the white shooting lodge on Middle Moor* (Peter Clowes).

Above April: *At first glance the dominant characteristics of the Dark Peak are the millstone grit rocks which give the area its name and ubiquitous heather* (Peter Clowes).

Middle May: *The willow warbler and its cousins fill the untainted air of May with joyous song out of all proportion to their size* (Sam Kennedy).

Right May: *There to be appreciated by those who will stop and look when walking in the Vosges are such delicate achievements of nature as the swallowtail butterfly* (Sam Kennedy).

May: *The phenomenon known as the Brocken Spectre is difficult to photograph successfully, but this attempt gives a fair impression of a fascinating spectacle* (Sam Kennedy).

May: *A perfect day for walking grants this view looking towards Baosbheinn from the Horns of Alligin* (Sam Kennedy).

Right June: *Late May and early June in the Pyrenees draws out such flowers as the dogstooth violet, a bright harbinger of summer* (Kev Reynolds).

Below June: *The lower Esera valley in June is warm, fragrant, colourful, remote and delightful* (Kev Reynolds).

ought to go through at night when the moon is 'at the full'. And Edward Bradbury, writing in 1884, described the dale as 'wild and savage' with the Wye 'wimpling on its way, sweeping in curves where the foam-bells swim round in joyful procession'.

Ahead lay another tunnel — this time its entrance sealed — at one of the most dramatic points of the dale where the railway pierced a bold limestone knoll. The Monsal Trail path turned off, dropping steeply through the oaks and willows to the river, which was tumbling wildly over a jumble of scattered boulders. I crossed a footbridge and walked on shingle at the side of the Wye under an overhanging precipice of limestone, its face scored with crooked, dripping fissures like the grooves on a well-used butcher's block. The river swirled along the foot of the cliff and the only way to proceed was along a line of large but uneven stepping stones — forty of them — that curved out of sight around a bend.

Luckily, the river was not in high flood condition — in winter the stones are frequently awash. On this April morning my feet remained dry. This was not the case, however, in April 1850 when William Adam, a Matlock geologist, found his way barred by 'an awful rocky chasm' that was 'fearful to look upon'. He and his companion were forced to clamber up the craggy side of the dale to safety. 'The river is hemmed in between perpendicular rocks', wrote the alarmed Adam, 'It is wholly impracticable for visitors... the heart quails'.

A moorhen strode through the shallows on its long legs on the far side of the river. Already, in anticipation of summer, vivid anemones and celandines were growing on the bank. Looming high above my head was the gaunt cliff of Chee Tor, 200 ft high, that juts into the gorge and forces the river to make a sharp U-turn. Small rivulets of water zig-zagged down its weathered face. Stunted bushes clung stubbornly to life in ragged clefts and ledges. It looked grim and lifeless, only sparingly tinged with lichens and moss.

The silence of the dale was soon broken by the chattering of a party of about fifty children, under the charge of four teachers, who were walking up the valley. I watched them jovially jostle each other to lead the way along the stepping stones and, when all was quiet again, stood immobile on the shingle as two chocolate-brown dippers alighted on a branch overhanging the river for a full minute before suddenly darting off up the stream.

Lower down the valley I abandoned the riverside path, which had become extremely rocky and frequently descended through masses of waist-high ferns into the shallows, to climb a flight of steps hewn out of the steep slope at the side of yet another viaduct and so regain the old trackbed high above the serpentine Wye. Green fields swept up towards a copse of sycamores perched on the skyline at the top of Chee Tor knoll.

A grassy path soon brought me to the site of Millers Dale Station, once an important junction for Buxton-bound passengers. Now there are few signs of this busy waypoint. One or two platforms emerge from the undergrowth, and the main building has been converted into a Peak Park ranger centre. There are useful toilets here as well.

The construction of a railway through this part of the Peak in 1863 meant mammoth engineering problems. Most Victorians thought railways the wonder of the age, but the desecration of the countryside that often resulted led to some opposition in the Press. After completion of the Millers Dale line John Ruskin commented bitterly: 'You blasted its rocks away, heaped thousands of tons of shale into its lovely stream. Now every fool in Buxton can be in Bakewell in half an hour and every fool in Bakewell at Buxton... you fools everywhere'.

When trains stopped running between Matlock and Peak Forest in 1968 it was hoped that the dales could be restored to their former condition. But the removal of so many viaducts, bridges and tunnel entrances would have been prohibitively expensive. In any case, the embankments had become covered with a hundred years' growth of trees and shrubs, which had softened their appearance. As a result the Monsal Trail — following the disused line from Topley Pike to just south of Bakewell — was conceived by the National Park.

From the ranger centre I walked down a B-road from Tideswell that crosses the river at Millers Dale and leaned over a wall to look back towards Chee Dale. Somewhere here in the early 19th century, when the Wye was crossed by a ford, the local squire, young William Bagshawe, and several of his men caught a group of poachers taking trout from the river at midnight. During the fight that followed in mid-stream William was killed.

Right *View of Monsal Dale viaduct and the trail which now runs over it, as seen from Monsal Head* (Peter Clowes).

Below right *The bridge at Upperdale* (Peter Clowes).

Five of the poachers were charged with murder, although all were later acquitted.

When James Croston, a Manchester rambler, visited the nearby Anglers' Rest Inn in 1870 he 'refreshed on oatcake and cheese — the only fare the humble larder could afford'. Time has apparently stood still in Millers Dale. When I walked into the pub, which stands close to the Wye, its entrance was festooned with notices. 'No boots allowed'. 'No dogs'. The barmaid dispensed cool beer but indicated that the only food available was a plain 'turkey cob'.

I walked on, taking a track that hugged the river bank between rough drystone walls. At Litton Mill, a huddle of low buildings that date from 1782, I recalled the working conditions facing pauper children 200 years ago, so vividly described in Walt Unsworth's novel *Devil's Mill*. Many of the youngsters, who were treated as nothing better than slaves, were buried at Tideswell Church, where their

graves can still be seen.

Great buttresses of rock now squeezed the river into a narrow high-walled passage and the path, dodging and twisting on a ledge along the north bank, was completely devoid of sunlight. More lilies grew on the water — on one pancake-sized leaf a whiskery water-vole sat contentedly washing itself — and there were patches of blue forget-me-not and bugle brightening the grass between clumps of wild rhubarb and cow parsley.

The Wye followed an S-shaped course through a deep defile known as Water-cum-Jolly. Cornices of rock, fringed with shrubs, protruded over my head on the tiny riverside path. At one bend a great sweep of trees filled the side of the gorge, climbing in row upon row to a lane leading to Litton village.

The water became more sluggish here, widening into a broad pool, and faint beams of sunlight made the creamy-green surface sparkle and glitter. I splashed through a flooded path under a curved cliff of smooth, slippery limestone and approached a low weir blocking the current. Beyond a rusty disused sluice gate stood the dilapidated remains of Cressbrook cotton mill, far different from its days of glory when the bell in its handsome cupola on the roof of the main block summoned people to work. Now the windows were gaping holes through which sparrows and starlings flew, the hands of the big clock high on the front wall were caked in slivers of rust.

Unlike Litton Mill up the valley, Cressbrook had a good reputation in the last century. Its owner, William Newton, a self-educated poet known as the Minstrel of the Peak, treated his workers well. 'In fine weather the children walked three miles to church in Tideswell', we are told by that intrepid Victorian travel writer J.B. Firth. 'In winter Sunday school was held in a large room at the mill'.

At the rear of the buildings I saw a stream tumbling down Cressbrook Dale and widening into a placid pool beneath a frieze of ash and beech before it poured into the Wye. This area is well-preserved by the Nature Conservancy. At one time large beds of mint, watercress and lilies of the valley were grown for the Manchester markets. Now the wood contains rare mosses and many exotic plants.

I stepped on to a substantial steel-beamed footbridge — erected by the Territorial Army in 1984 — and crossed the river next to the wild thundering weir. In the narrow gorge below the barrier the water foamed like milk boiling violently in a giant's saucepan. From here a level path across the green shoulder of High Field rejoined the Monsal Trail where the former rail track emerged from Cressbrook Tunnel. The path, thickly flanked by silver birch and willow, now followed a ledge gouged out of the rock along the side of Monsal Dale, the river below flowing through meadows as the valley widened. Longstone Edge lay to the north, the white-walled fields under its escarpment rocks sulking in a pale blue haze.

Two hundred yards below my feet a sturdy iron-railed footbridge crossed the deep, green, swirling waters of the Wye as the path neared Monsal Head. Years ago the bridge was of rustic wooden planks resting on rough piles of stones — one to 'delight the soul of a painter', according to M.J.B. Baddeley — but, after it had been swept away several times, the present structure was erected. Near it stands a neat farmhouse. Two white horned goats were tethered in a side paddock, one of them on its hind legs chewing the leaves of an apple tree. Two dogs — fortunately securely chained — barked furiously as a group of ramblers walked

past the farm gate towards the bridge.

I could no longer resist the lure of the river, which was now widening and sweeping in a graceful curve through the arches of Monsal Dale Viaduct, and I followed a path down to the thistle-crowded waterside meadows. Two walkers with heavy binoculars around their necks met me. They had been looking intently at several birds fluttering in the branches of an alder on the far bank. 'Long-tailed tits', said the man finally. 'And we have just seen a treecreeper.' It was obviously a good April day for birdwatching. In fact, as we talked, great-crested grebe, mallard and coot splashed into sight on the river.

The well-known railway viaduct, on which Edward Bradbury saw 'the flash of a Pullman car' before it plunged into Headstone Tunnel, has slim piers and graceful arches of mixed limestone and grey brick. Its appearance today is far from appealing but, as a piece of industrial architecture, it somehow fits into the pattern of the landscape with remarkable style and is now a listed building.

This part of Monsal Dale, where the river is forced to bend at right angles against the solid massif of Monsal Head, has attracted tourists for more than 100 years. So many, in fact, that the Midland Railway built a small station nearby, using wooden piles (which can still be seen) to secure an outer platform on the hillside.

My path kept to the bank of the river. White water was plunging over the mossy, weed-draped, stone steps of a weir and a breeze blowing up the valley was creating a hazy cloud of fine spray. Sheep grazed amid the trees and on the open slope of Putwell Hill behind my back. A man who had walked down from Monsal Head was hurling a branch into the water for his Alsatian dog to retrieve. Another man, elderly, frail-looking, stumbling along the path in green wellingtons with the aid of a stick, told me he had parked his car at the Monsal Head Hotel. 'I live in the Hope Valley seven miles away,' he said. 'I come down here for a short walk most days. It's paradise.'

I crossed the river by a footbridge — the last crossing place for more than two miles — and climbed a well-maintained path over tree-roots and slippery rocks through thick woodland that covers the northern slope of Fin Cop. There were patches of mire and rutty hollows worn by rills trickling down the hillside. The deafening roar of the weir faded astern and I did not pause until the path crossed the hill high above the river and immediately over the end of the viaduct.

The vale was spread out in a vast panorama of fields, river, woods and undulating hills. Blue smoke from a farmhouse curled up the grassy slopes, the Wye rippled between the legs of cattle standing in the cool water, two magpies swooped over a tractor chugging along the lane, sheep seemed to be everywhere.

April, however, is a very unpredictable month. Grey clouds were filling the valley above Cressbrook and spots of rain were beginning to fall as I walked into the car park at Monsal Head. There was a welcoming coal fire in the hotel's old-fashioned bar, which had a fine plaster ceiling and Victorian prints on the walls. Threakston's bitter and excellent snacks provided by the affable bearded landlord enticed one to linger but the day was over and I had a problem — getting back to Topley Pike. Derbyshire miles, though full of interest, can sometimes be very long miles!

Peter Clowes has been hill-walking throughout Britain since his teens. He was born in a Derbyshire farmhouse, is a frequent visitor to the Peak District (on the borders of which he and his wife live) and is a regular contributor to countryside magazines. A professional journalist and former newspaper editor, his interests include fly-fishing for trout in the Derbyshire rivers, steam trains (wherever they can be found) and every aspect of rural nostalgia.

Three sides of May

SAM KENNEDY

Jealousy, plain and simple, impelled me to make for Torridon. Isobel's bubbling enthusiasm for Liathach after a recent splendid summer traverse brightened an otherwise unspectacular autumn day on Beinn Eunaich and Beinn a' Chochuill. There and then, my long May weekend was settled. It just had to be Torridon! Like most 'expeditions', there was a period of ferment as plans were formulated. Compromised itineraries to quell threats of divorce proceedings and the sordid machinations to determine who gets custody of the cat — these traumas haunt any self-respecting climber or rambler. Eventually, still married, I set off with a colleague from work on a Thursday late in May.

The drive to Torridon from Loch Lomond took almost six hours and served to dispirit us somewhat. Rain, less rain, more rain, threats of rain, spots of rain and a uniformly grey sky all the way from Spean Bridge. It was nothing if not typically Scottish. Glencoe had worn one of its dark scowls, growling 'Wha daur meddle wi' me?' in its inimitable forbidding way. Is there comparable majesty in any Scottish valley? A rhetorical question, surely?

Other valleys may compete with its fearsome pinnacles and buttresses, gigantic corries, rare and varied flora and fauna and overall size, but where else are you dwarfed thus from both north and south in an extensive tract of valley floor? Glen Brittle radiates magnificence at a distance from the east. The great glens of the Cairngorms lack an Aonach Eagach. Even of stately Glen Etive, it must be said, *proxime accessit*. The Coe need fear no false pretender.

I stray, however, from the subject in hand. In Torridon, too, there rise other shrines aplenty before which we worship with sweat, endeavour and wonder. Ours was an inauspicious arrival. Having stopped to give a lift to two other 'pilgrims' returning from Beinn Eighe, the car stalled and refused to re-start — it was quickly rectified but it was the first of two small snags during our stay.

Camp was pitched between Liathach and

Beinn Eighe, and plans were made for an early start. Hitch number two could have been nasty, but the fates were with me. The grey sky, darkening, suddenly became suffused with blue — no meteorological miracle, just cursing, wailing and despicable ill-temper when I realized that I had not packed my sleeping-bag. Davy came to the rescue with a spare light summer bag, and most welcome it was, since there was overnight frost.

A shake of snow fell on Liathach at first light, accentuating its massive frame, and the eastern extremity looked even more vertical than it had on our approach some hours before. Its steepness presents no major challenge as we found on gritting our teeth for the initial ascent to Stuc a'Choire Dhuibh Bhig in worsening weather: wind-driven sleet for twenty minutes was more discouraging than the obstacles to our gaining the ridge. Once on top, we were tormented by mist denying us views of the expanse of Torridon and its ridges and corries. So close we knew was the quartzite of Eighe, yet it might as well have been galaxies distant.

The visibility remained tantalizingly low from Bidean Toll a'Mhuic to Spidean a'Choire Leith, and the way over the Am Fasarinen pinnacles offered only momentary glimpses of Coire na Caime. Then, miraculously, the sleet and wind had gone. We neared Mullach an Rathain, and like a biblical revelation, the mists parted and spread a tapestry of sea, spring green and scree before us.

Odd tenacious patches of snow persisted here and there. Having spun round the corries either side of the Northern Pinnacles, banks of mist threatened to rejoin ranks almost as quickly as they had cleared. We chose to avoid the remaining tops — a judicious decision, since heavy rain followed shortly after the spell of blue and sparkling sunshine. The weather-map that Jack could have built: frost by night, snow at dawn, sleet and wind, damp mists, forceful sunshine and clear skies all washed down with a final deluge, a patchwork of

Liathach from the boulder field of Beinn Eighe (Sam Kennedy).

pleasures to greet our first outing. Bowing to the demands of decency, and scorning the weak degeneracy of the flesh, no mention will be made of the ensuing soirée.

There being for every action an equal and opposite reaction, the grunts and bleary eyes rendered us unfit to meet the breaking of such a special day as the next. The morning had the clarity of a well-reasoned argument. The rising sun seemed cooled by the sharp, tingling cold. It struggled to break from the vice of this abrasive chill, warm the atmosphere and stamp its vital presence on the earth.

A scant breakfast — always a folly — then we took the path once more for Coire Dubh Mor, branching north onto the chunky quartzite. The rocky slopes of Beinn Eighe to the south-east of A'Choinneach Mhor proved unsteady, forcing a rhythm of two steps forward and one back and much changing of direction. On reaching the broad ridge, we veered north-westwards to A'Choinneach Mhor, and opted firstly for the northern spur to Ruadh-stac Mor.

Clouds spawned from nowhere, clichés of cotton-wool, burgeoning without menace, and needlessly serving to enhance the already wondrous picture of gargantuan terraces, pyramids, and wedges of sandstone. Below this profile of Liathach from the north there stretched the long glistening stream Abhainn Coire Mhic Nobuil, a silver thread unwinding from the reel of lochans in upper Coire Mhic Nobuil.

Panoramic views of Torridon's rich landscape could not be far away. We pressed on and stopped where the ridge drops slightly before Ruadh-stac Mor. In some ways this is a disappointing top, too flat and rounded a first lady for this White House. From a vantage point above the celebrated Coire Mhic Fhearcair, the immense triple buttresses could be admired; huge lithops with runnels of scree dropping like roots to feed from the waters of Loch Coire Mhic Fhearcair — a fanciful image, no doubt, of this inorganic life. They are, in reality, towering rock-faces destined to be gnawed eternally by the north and west winds, insidiously undermined by ice and rain for aeons, hammered on the anvil of the elements

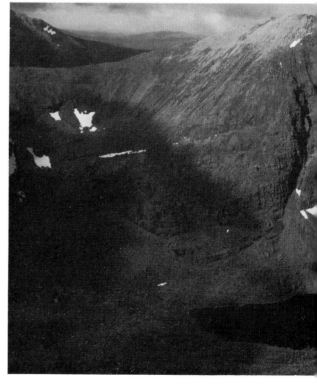

for innumerable millenia after the demise of man. It seems presumptuous to seek to evoke the atmosphere and define the stature of something so immense.

We retraced our steps to gain A'Choinneach Mhor from Ruadh-stac Mor. Swinging towards Sail Mhor along the wide, lush, mossy ridge, flecked with alpine plants, we disturbed a solitary male dotterel. This is the highest-nesting of all British breeding wading birds. Late May and June is their normal breeding time, but these are birds usually associated with the extensive plateaux of the Grampians or Cairngorms over 2,500 ft, not the sharp-ridged western peaks.

For this odd little bird, the chances of breeding success on this oasis of flattish terrain were slim. The female dotterel is the avian reader of *Spare Rib* — she is polyandrous, laying more than one clutch of eggs and flirting with more than one male. The male, however, hatches the eggs and tends the brood. He distracts enemies with elaborate displays: amongst other actions, he feigns injury to a wing to lure predators away from the young. Our dotterel merely disappeared behind slight hummocks of moss and lichen, and we did not harass him.

Beyond the rise of verdant sub-alpine garden lay the route to Sail Mhor, altogether more splendid than Ruadh-stac Mor. From this lower top, there is a circle of magnificent views to peaks whose very names enthrall — Liathach, Alligin, Baosbheinn, and distant An Teallach. As always on Scotland's western seaboard, a fringe of ocean exerted an almost magnetic pull: mesmerizing landscapes abounded from this beautiful outlying peak, an honorary Munro. To reach Sail Mhor involves moderate, interesting scrambling on leaving and returning to the ridge topping the Triple Buttresses.

Much to-ing and fro-ing, and we were once more on A'Choinneach Mhor set to head east for Spidean Coire nan Clach. Between these peaks thrift flowered, deeper red than I'd ever seen, a mellow light burgundy amidst the dazzling quartzite. Spreading mountain thyme reached out to colonize further, and delicate slender-stalked saxifrages shook in the sporadic

Sail Mhor and Lochan Coire Mhic Fhearchair, the most dramatic contrast one could ask for (Sam Kennedy).

In May the common snipe can, with care, be caught at nest with her chicks (Sam Kennedy).

swishes of tepid breeze. To the south, in the direction of Beinn Liath Mhor, a Golden eagle swirled in high, wide circles — so distant that a blink forced re-focussing to follow its lazy sweeps.

Coire Mhic Fhearcair must satisfy the romantic — a lochan, its waters replenished by avalanche and snow–melt, it is almost encircled by sheer rock walls whose essence superlatives fail to capture. It brims to saturate the boggy moorland, sodden tangles of heather, low reeds and mossy mounds where snipe raise their families: gorgeous, gangly-legged chicks, russet, chocolate-brown and spangling-eyed, vulnerable fluff-balls on leathery stilts. The moorland is veined with burns, broad, galloping and uncrossable in spate or mild trickling mumbles. Their tributaries swell from deep sphagnum-lined holes, coagulated in the parching swelter of high summer, plugged with ice in mid-winter, a-swirl and flowing between these extremes of seasonal variation. Moorland: mystical, often featureless terrain, a refuge for the natural and unhusbanded. Coire Mhic Fhearcair lords over such glories and nods acquaintance with the peaks of the Flowerdale Forest.

The ridge-walking became even grander approaching Spidean Coire nan Clach: bearings north and south led in turn down precipitous crags and steep slopes. Beinn Eighe has two other northern corries. Seen from the ridge, these are spacious quasi-lunar craters splashed with earthly green. The more easterly of them seems at once broad and sprawling, with configurations of sea-scape, in places an enlarged model of a child's comb-painting. It is high and crumbling too: elevation is lent by that great decaying molar crowned by Sgurr nan Fhir Duibhe.

From Sgurr Ban moribund snow patches seemed just to resist the onslaught of May's mildness. Cloud-filtered sunrays blotched the ragged rock-faces. Coral-like, in shadow and light, they contrasted with the evenly lit light-grey arc of scree before them. Menacing stumps of stone and v-shaped gouges lay between us and the completion of the west-east traverse. We dipped to the col after Sgurr Ban and wound ourselves up physically and mentally for another push to yet one more summit.

Perception and reality made their not inhabitual divergence when the pinnacles

Left *Configurations of sea-scape — looking north-east from Sgurr Ban* (Sam Kennedy).

Below *Sgurr nan Fhir Duibhe, a dominant and impressive ridge which always demands respect* (Sam Kennedy).

materialized as enjoyable, moderate scrambles.
We gazed irresistibly over the cliffs, down
gradations of broken-toothed rock, ledges of
crumbled stone and labyrinths of weaving
sunlight and deep shade to the corrie floor. To
the west were the spurs from Spidean Coire
nan Clach: on the north-east, a bisecting
division between Ruadh-stac Mor and Creag
Dhubh; south-eastwards, a natural approach
from, or descent route to, Glen Torridon.

The glass is never empty, but we had
quaffed our fill, sipped of the timeless and
colossal. Intoxicated, we now deserted the
ptarmigan, resident percussionist of the
mountain orchestra. Its rasping cries, atonal
and barren, complement its preferred haunts:
to us, harsh, exacting and mercurial in
disposition; to it, plentiful pastures. From
Creag Dhubh we crossed Coire Domhain and
came to a long stone-shoot. The echoes of the
high top drowned in the gushing songs of
skylark and meadow-pipit. Mountain ceded to
moorland, roseroot to sundew. The brew may
have been heady — it was certainly addictive.

Larks rose with the promise of dawn.
Heather was back-lit by the glow of the
emergent sun — good omens for our last day.
Beyond the dapple of oak, birch and pine lay
Alligin: prostrate, its flank smitten in mortal
fray, like a slain reptilian Goliath. Headless, it
was slumped by the loch's depths, whence,
apparently, it had lumbered to its doom.

Our mood was exultant. Map and compass
were tucked redundant in our sacks. Profiting
from the sparkling, cloudless morning, we took
the crow's route to the summit of Beinn Dearg.
The simile changed image and became
metaphor. The ascent of Beinn Dearg was now
our aperitif, and the banquet was set before us.
Appetites would be whetted on *hors d'oeuvres*
Horns of Alligin. The main course was Terrine
Sgurr Mhor, served with a side salad of
Baosbheinn and Beinn an Eoin. Nor would
dessert Tom na Gruagaich occasion
disappointment. The wines too were vintage: a
vin du pays, Château Loch a'Bhealaich,
necessarily unpretentious when followed by
the stunning Première Cuvée Château
Atlantique Eternelle. The metaphor allowed
itself a snigger — this was *haute cuisine*! In
anticipation, we offered our compliments to
the chef. Regrettably, we did not catch the
name, and doubtless never will.

By mid-morning, the shameful mistreatment
of Beinn Dearg was over. We had accorded it

no status, yet it is a hill worthy of much more
than the philistinism of a direct ascent and
descent. On the Torridon family tree, it is a
full cousin to Liathach, Eighe and Alligin. It
was after all Sunday, and from Beinn Dearg, all
three family elders wore their best.

Singlemindedly, we proceeded down and
over the valley, across Allt a'Bhealaich to tackle
the Horns of Alligin. With hindsight, the verb
was inappropriate. They offered no contest,
were sparring partners rather than opponents.
The climb was a waltz, not the all too familiar
military two-step. However, it was May, it was
mild, and the sun was invigorating. Flotillas of
miniature clouds passed languidly over from
north and west; here a patchy gauze of
shadow, there robust sunlight over the moor.
Gloss changed to matt: Loch a'Ghobhain a
lustrous blue, Loch Toll nam Biast inky, whilst
Loch a'Bhealaich mirrored both. Baosbheinn's
humps faded from brown to fawn; the slopes
were tinged with olive-green.

The landscape was compulsive, so
distractingly lovely, that lapses in
concentration were both inevitable and
excusable. We reached Sgurr Mhor in one
piece and, being Scottish, set to devouring
another. More accurately, lunch was a chewing
of cud: in the reverie of tastes and thoughts,
foreground blurred to horizon, then sharpened
again into clear relief. Impertinently placed,
mock conquerors, we looked onto the warty
spine of the imagined antediluvian beast. The
charms of Torridon's Liathach and Eighe
became extensions of the simile, petrified
vestiges of ancient animal form. All the while
too, infinitely westwards, the ocean had
beckoned, more concept than physical entity.
Mountains exude power and breadth, yet they
have parameters. Ocean apes them but has
none. A mountain is a fly in the amber of time,
an ocean a disembodied spirit more akin to
that fourth dimension that is past, present and
future.

We came round and had soon covered the
gap to Tom na Gruagaich. We had failed to
notice billboards in the village posted with
news of this Highland gathering — or was it
some ... rock concert? Nevertheless, crowds
there were, of people and dogs. With the usual
oiling of social wheels, nods, smiles and
mumbled greetings, our brief stop on Tom na
Gruagaich ended, and likewise, our visit to
Alligin and Torridon drew to a close. The
crescendos of the past three days echoed to us

Looking back over the Horns of Alligin to Beinn Dearg, Beinn Eighe and Liathach (Sam Kennedy).

as we passed down through Coire nan Laoigh to return to base and prepare for the diminuendo of departure.

From seeds sown thus ripen harvests of memories, ears or sackfuls for the granary of the subconscious. Be it a stand of wild orchids flooded with sunlight, cherry-red stars of marsh cinquefoil, or the warp and weft of sky and land, recollections are ingots in the mind's vault. Down the path, on occasion, there strides a familiar and welcome stranger. Such are my memories of Torridon. I shall reciprocate soon, I hope, by returning.

On an evening in May by the Lang Crags, the local name for the Kilpatrick hills, we met a shepherd: a Sophist, modern-day purveyor of warped logic, he was himself a walker, but scornful of the breed. To him we were Goth or Vandal bent on plunder, and, straight through the tunnel of his mind came an accusatory shaft of philosophical light.

'Ye're either gaun' tae trouble or comin' frae it.' Remonstrations that we were *bona fide* hikers, protestations of our innocence of past act or future criminal intent — no reasonable argument could find a chink in the armour of his illiberalism until a flash of inspiration: 'Did ye know Jock Cochrane?' He had known my grandfather, a ploughman in these parts. Drip by drip the thaw started, and he spoke of the wildlife, but rarely in other than pejorative terms. His Weltblick owed more to cant than Kant. We wondered whether he or we should have been called on to produce credentials, though we parted on amicable terms.

The path skirted the crags and led towards Doughnut hill. Wheatears flitted among the rounded boulders and skylarks rose and sang and rose and sang, and sang and sang... This is Overtoun, the start of our journey: pleasant green country bordered by moorland on the east, overlooking the Clyde on the west where it heads to the firth and the sea: the northern vista is Loch Lomond and the southernmost

Scottish Highlands, our destination. I do not intend autobiography. However, my proposed itineraries recall the parochial adventure-packed years of a life which has seen me leave my native Dumbarton for that edge of a local boy's universe, Balloch, via the not-so-sleepy hamlet of Renton.

From Overtoun House towards Loch Bowie, branching west over Barnhill will lead steeply and pleasantly down to the outskirts of Dumbarton. Set off, and in the paucity of trees before the Giant's Staircase to the Crags, the green woodpecker's derisory mix of squeal and yell is sometimes heard. In May, cuckoo flowers mass in the fields, and on the dam, a choked and reedy pond, 'where weeds in wheels shoot long and lovely and lush' the dabchicks tend their first brood. This smallest of our native grebes sports one light spot between its beak and eye, its plumage otherwise is dark or glossy chestnut browns. On this rich and shining moss green lochan, they spend from spring to summer, self-sufficient.

Along the Leven banks dusk is close as you pass the willows on the bend, and there is a smooth flow between the whirlpools south of Kilmalid and the ebb-tide rapids where the reed-beds lie opposite. Trout are rising: a cloudless rainfall on the river, they suck down the sun-hatched flies or leap in a frenzy and splash to seize their chosen prey in flight. With stilted mid-air twists and gauche, buckling turns, they are fish out of water. In the aftermath glow of sunset you stroll home and could vow to the heresy that there is no winter.

A heavenly host of swifts confirms your conversion. They too are non-believers in this orthodoxy. With evangelical zeal they fly in a scything rush and net the insect shoals with jubilant screams. They bolt unbridled in a sleek wheel of flight from the eaves of the old town's sandstone tenements, and hawk over the river, high above where once were tidal swamps and spears of reed.

Return to the river bank at first light and, overnight, spiders have spun shimmering fragile rounds of silk. These fishermen of the dawn have dew-hung nets, but trap not trawl. You exhale and are aware of breathing, and the river is silent till you come once more to the early simmer of rising trout and the cauldron of spinning river beyond. Here all roads can lead you to roam. Cross to the west bank,

For the observant there are such floral delights as the wood sorrel (Sam Kennedy).

however, and follow the path past Dalquhurn, redolent of industrial dereliction and dilapidation. There is still enterprise here, a thriving business in joint names, directors the venerable Barn-Owls, Makers of Fine Soft Fluffy Toys. The migrant spotted flycatchers breed nearby at the loop on the river, hunting bees and wasps with relentless fervour. We have reached the village of Renton, an idyllic aspect once, before the Industrial Revolution. On the hill off west above the 'Hundred Steps' is Carman moor, beyond the edge of deciduous woodland stretching from Dalmoak and the Kipperoch. A path through the woods will take us there.

'For lo the winter is past, the rain is over and gone;

The flowers appear on the earth; the time of the singing of the birds is come, and the voice

of the turtle is heard in our land' — *The Song of Solomon*

In the valley of the Leven, rain may mock and defy the seasons and the warm, hoarse and nasal calls of woodpigeon never mingle with 'the voice of the turtle', but May is 'the time of the singing of the birds': a fertile time, a time of significance, of the magnum opus of regeneration; it is the time of woodland's grand opera. The set is fashioned of oak and birch, beech and ash and holly, inlaid with tangles of grass and bramble, adorned with twining honeysuckle and the wax-leaved limpet ivy, all spring-cleansed to bluebell-bright, speckled with the sorrels and anemones of the wood.

You need not walk far to gather and hoard the frequently lost treasures of the dawn, watch day shake off the black and smothering night, and hear that 'fine careless rapture'. An apparent ecstasy, a *joie de vivre*, belies the purposeful menace of birdsong: an array of caveats and expletives masquerading in

melody, sweetness veiling aggression. This is no idiotic bravado. Never were the bugle-bursts of warring factions more tuneful, more spontaneous, more necessary.

May is a punctual month, a spruce and dapper visitor, fresh, green and scrubbed new. It does not arrive in a puffing bluster like March, or find itself dishevelled, caught in squalls and showers as April. It comes laden with plenty, and bids us warm welcome.

Between the wood and the moor, Small Tortoiseshells are about, palettes of colour on their wings, orange-red, black, brown and white and blue: gaudiest and commonest of butterflies in the valley, they are often confused with the Red Admirals, a species more obviously dotted and splotched with white. On the moor, among the gorse spikes, diminutive Green Hairstreaks are unmistakable. Butterflies flap, sail and tack, buoyed by the warmth of late spring. They use the following winds from now through summer to cross the oceans of the year, depositing a future at port, among the banks of flowers.

The moor has foxes, the moor has owls, the moor has lizards, but the moor has also curlews. Words can tell of beautiful ringing, bubbling wells of song and wild strident cries. Their true wildness, true tones and true pitch are somehow things only of the moor itself. Not confined to moorland, they breed throughout Scotland, but winter on the coast. In early May they will have eggs, olive, four in number and hidden in a nest among the heather. Curlews are the epitome of this marshy moorland, 'crying their cries of creatures never tame'. We round Carman Dam to head north along the valley flank for Stoneymollan. Bog-bean and asphodel are budded and tormentil everywhere.

Think now of deception, of opportunism, of an eye open to the main chance. Think of breaking and entering, of swinish indifference and of fraudulent disguise. She stands accused of these and more: charged with crimes against the state, the human moral state. Her plea is diminished responsibility. She is illegitimate, has never known her parents, had been fostered at birth. Counsel warns that she is a repeated offender. Nevertheless the sentence must be lenient: her deeds are only the cuckoo's sad efficiency. Her calls pervade the moor.

At Carman Dam, land on the north-east is tilled and, over the moor, some few acres

Above *The common lizard enjoys the spring sunshine* (Sam Kennedy).

Right *A curlew returns to the nest as evening falls* (Sam Kennedy).

south, it is reclaimed to a damp depression. From here it rises and dries in a parabola over to the farm at Kipperoch. These marginal lands are planted or grazed and house all you would expect — brown hares and rabbits, peewits and oystercatchers. Our thoughts are re-diverted to the moorland marsh north of the Dam and the hillside beyond. The valley on the west of the Leven rises to a broad ridge. This we avoid, preferring the valley-side. It is indented with tiny narrow burns and ditches and occasional flower-rich wetland. Bugle and orchids and violets nestle among the grasses and quills of reed and the pearl-bordered fritillaries rest their stained-glass wings. Redpolls nest where moorland and farmland meet, and roe deer slip furtively back into the thick quietness of the wood as we approach.

The woodland below accompanies us to Stoneymollan. The shallow cuts into the hillside deepen, forming high-banked clefts topped with rowans. Ahead are broader corrugations before we descend to the stream then move uphill past the splendid beech-row. At last we stand among Scots pines and larch, our view to the loch and mountains once more unimpaired.

Loch Lomond laps round dark-forested islands showered in the falling melody of willow warblers. It breaks in foam on shores where oak-woods resound with drumming great-spotted woodpeckers and effervescent bursts of wood warbler song. It rocks to please the wind: scoters and mergansers bob and dip in time, 'and the May month flaps its glad green leaves like wings'. Tranquil it may be too, the islands unruffled, an enchantment of glades and coverts and thickets, drowsy and still on the fine May days.

Winter can lurk in the spring mountains. Rock and rain and earth are welded by cold to an icy conglomerate. Till May, night and frosts will stem the thaw. May is the turnkey to winter's lock. The release swells the streams, unlocks and stirs the start to flourishing summer. Ben Lomond may be revived to a great green mountain. Often still it bears the not uncommon 'snow in May's new-fangled mirth'. These lands are stalked by uncertainty.

Had we spurned the young man's path west at Kilmalid and left the river, we should have followed the tributary east against the current. By the river a cock reed bunting is hooded in

The female redpoll on her nest is a faithful parent, resentful of intrusion (Sam Kennedy).

Right and below *Ben Lomond belies its size and serious walking possibilities on a warm day in May* (Sam Kennedy).

The dipper, here bringing food to the nest, is a dashing sight on upland rivers in May (Sam Kennedy).

black: it guards the secret whereabouts of its scribbled eggs. The portly dipper lands on a rock, genuflects, submerges and reappears successful. It flies to a perch then on to its nest with the food. A pun would have its life a busy round. In the calm shallows are those shrunken monsters, newts; while sticklebacks parade and procreate in the quiet of deeper pools.

On up through the glen past the Murroch farm, the way is by the fields north or south, or to continue to alter course with the burn. The views from above the glen are onto the crowns of statuesque oaks and beeches, a sanctuary cherished by the small song-birds. Chaffinch, song and mistle thrushes, blackbirds and wren all breed here. The walk through the glen is unsurpassable as beams of sunlight penetrate the leaf-cover: they light the woodland breaks or sparkle at the touch of water.

The rare nightjar has been heard churring from the fern-fields east of the valley, but twilight rouses the tawny owls to harvest a crop of voles and mice and make provision for their chicks. I have not heard nightjars. I have, however, spent whole nights in May, when greenshanks passed overhead on migration, watching the tawny owl return with food. She stores a larder in an austere hollow of nest, a gruesome cellar laid down against inclement weather. I have seen the birth of the owlets, emerging rude pink and plucked. Weeks later, their white plumage starts to shade over to light brown.

We have come to the canyonous upper reaches of the Murroch glen. We turn north across the broad sweep of moorland risen with knolls, half marsh, half heather. On the east, the river valley joins the hill-top, flattening into moorland. There are some birches half-way, and long-eared owls frequent the place. We can drop to the valley or continue to the Scots pine woods lying beyond the fields east of Balloch. Only here on a May morning and on the ridge-top of An Teallach above the A'Mhaighdean wilderness have I ever seen the Brocken Spectre. Your shadow is cast eerily and disconcertingly into the mist — a phenomenon giving rise no doubt to chimerical fancies. A redshank calls from over the rounded hill. They come with plover, curlew and sandpiper, from the sea or the south, and dash colour on the moor. Their calls and songs, their shapes and flight are so many facets of 'the million-petalled flower of being'.

Through the entrance west of the gates are few trees and dense undergrowth before we enter the heart of Balloch Park. Weasels squirm through the low cover to terrify their prey. Soon there will be candles of greater butterfly orchid on the uncut grasslands, and alders on the riverside have followed the early catkins with a display of deep-green leaves. Beyond the park close by the water are old, old birch trees, thick-trunked, with crusts of lichen. Globeflower and water avens thrive beside the channels where the loch encroaches in winter: the yellow iris is tight with buds. The elders are youthful beside the elder statesmen in this wooded parliament, the upper house of birches. A mile or two along the loch, the shore-side has thin films of water and smooth, protruding stones: opposite lies Inchmurrin, most southerly of the islands. We complete our journey in Boturich, above the loch and beneath the mountains. Many have travelled far for this!

Journeys are incomplete without memories. On May evenings I walk often to Boturich to stand by the field beyond the pond and admire...simply admire. The day had been clear then cloudy then clear, bright and dull and bright. The sun was leaving by way of the Luss hills to rise again in the Far East — the other side of the world. Its farewell was a dragon-breath sunset, flames of lemon and yellow, of orange and red. Contortions of fine cloud formed ribs and filaments and objects of the imagination. A woodcock flew to proclaim a stake in the land, drawing its invisible plans. Day had faded to night in melting embers across the sky and the mountains lay dark and still and dead. Morning would work a miracle.

The river was rising to spate as we drove along Glen Etive: the rain was a heavy drizzle and thickening. Spring was thrawn and dree, dug in against summer's siege: Scottish spring in the invisible mountains. The glen was grey above green as May drenched Ben Starav's north ridge and all else besides. Buachaille Etive Beag

Who would deny the greater butterfly orchid a place in paradise? (Sam Kennedy).

was a whale-back but did not surface all day — we were the Jonahs! By late next day I was to be in other hills, west of Alsace and the Rhine. Over the Grand Ballon d'Alsace to La Bresse was my entry to the Vosges. West of the vineyards, orchards and farmlands of Alsace, south-east of the industrial cities of Metz and Nancy and north and east of 'la petite Norvège', little Norway, *la Haute Saône* — these are the Vosges mountains. I made a *faux pas*. I called them '*collines*' (hills) and almost shattered a recently signed *entente cordiale*. Furthermore, in the face of contrary opinion, I stoutly maintained that they were hills. The spring-to-autumn hills do become winter mountains.

The Vosges are a maze of valleys and still lakes: winding valleys which snake and fork; lakes in the depths of forests, screened by the tallest of trees. The pine-woods have companion beech and spruce, and in their semi-shade are fronds of unfurled ferns, wild

The Vosges (mountains) and the Vosges (hills): summer and winter in May (Sam Kennedy).

On trails the common toad is a familiar wayside friend (Sam Kennedy).

rose and forest fruits. The roe-buck moves, foraging from frame to frame of pine. Wild boars will wallow somewhere by the woods, and white-faced hook-horned chamois walk over the rough, rocky ground above or by the tree-line.

From above La Bresse I looked to Cornimont, then east towards the Hohneck as the night flew into a white temper. Whiplashes of light flailed the woods and settlements, penetrated the shutters, and dimmed again to blackness. Thunder pounded through the mountains, engulfing the silence. Greater than the roar and rage of a storm-swollen ocean against cliffs, a sky-quake, it broke the atmosphere in eruptions of grinding creaks and cracks, like the snapping masts of a million tall-ships. The tide of morning refloated shipwrecked night. Oh to be in Scotland now that spring was here!

It was by now mid-week and I was free, free to walk. Roads zig-zag almost to the tops of the Vosges and cross in places from valley to valley at cols where the forests split. There are so many beaten tracks, but on top, the spirit of places to wander is restored. I lived on the north-western valley-side between two forests, the Forêt de Cornimont and the Forêt de

Noiregoutte. Beneath, the Moselotte left the mountains to join the Moselle east of Remiremont.

I set off for Moutier des Fées, the high point on the north-west: literally 'the fairies' monastery', actually a few huge boulders prominent above the pines with views to forever. Water tunnels dribbled through the meadows, preparing for the June festival of Alpine lady's mantle and forget-me-not. The hillside was a series of sloping pasture-lands, a day-time Milky Way of flowers. By a low waterfall on Basses des Feignes a toad had purpose in mind, undecipherable purpose, and above, a goshawk flew the forest edge to foray and pursue. My questions to Vosgiens about the birds and the bees had been treated with a parental admonition:

... faut pas les toucher!' ('You must not touch them!')

Nothing but *fau(x/t) pas*! The ubiquitous globeflowers of Loch Lomondside were hallowed rarities here, hence the concern.

From field to path to field my route was indefinite, and as I came within sight of the summit, blaeberry and beech scrub greeted my wandering eye. The walk had been a spectrum through green, lime-light to pine-needle deep.

The globeflower, a familiar sight in Scotland, is rare in the Vosges (Sam Kennedy).

In flounced a debutante in a graceful float of self-important poise. Flirting with her hosts, the beeches, the Swallowtail danced the day away. Her ball-gown was in woven silks of black and yellow and sequin scales of blue: interludes were spent on a *chaise longue* of beech-leaf low to the ground. Undulations of valley and forest lay in waves before me. This calm had never heard of last night's storm.

My visit straddled May and June and my time shortened as the days lengthened. Spring would soon change without ceremony to summer. I crossed the river to the meadows on the east where peacock butterflies would glide among nettles on my return in early September. From the south-west I approached Lac des Corbeaux ('Crows' Lake'), a long march on a high forest path. Where were the crows? Even blacker were the birds I saw. In the Vosges names often have a German tinge, more marked as you move east through Alsace. The German name for the Lesser Grey Shrike is as sinister a condemnation as exists. '*Der Schwarzstirnwürger*' (the black-browed strangler) breeds nearby in the hawthorn, and compounds its seeming horrid deeds by impaling a stock of putrefying carcasses on thorns. *Chacun à son goût*!

I left the Vosges reluctantly, unaware then of winter's drifts and arms of pine-branch laden to submission with a welter of frosted snow. The Vosges were in blossom from valley to peak, through meadow and forest. Emissaries from the Moutier des Fées had spelled summer over winter, transformed the mountains to hills again in a trance of heat and long light.

Sam Kennedy was born in Dumbarton and educated at Dumbarton Academy and Glasgow University. He lives by Loch Lomondside and teaches in Erskine. He has walked and climbed in Scotland, the Vosges and the Alps and regularly lectures on ornithology, mountaineering and photography.

June in the Pyrenees

KEV REYNOLDS

In the lowlands June bursts with a vibrancy all its own. Since the release of winter's dark hold on the landscape it seems the countryside has been building steadily to a pitch that is about to be fulfilled. Its evidence is all around us.

Meadows have become heady with pollen. They are lush and overblown, jungle-rich with insect life; grasses stand waist-high and patterned with long-stemmed flowers growing tall as they stretch up for the light; feathery seed-heads ripe for finches, hillsides loud with the stitching of grasshoppers. The hiccup of the cuckoo may soon be gone, but toward evening squadrons of low-flying swifts, swallows and martins race screeching round farms and barns and village houses, swooping on midges caught unawares by the madness of midsummer.

There is a drumming pulse of life that beats its frenetic rhythm throughout the month of June. You can feel it in the air as much as hear it. It's as evident as the sun's warmth, for it is born of the sun: a rhythm set by the metronome of summer. Midsummer. Full sun, early mornings, late evenings. A long twilight reluctance by day to make way for night. An unmistakable energy reverberating through the countryside. Scent and sound reaching a climax that July will no doubt attempt to stifle. June is rich, light, airy. It's a time to be out early in the dew-cool of daybreak, pacing the world with eyes and ears and nostrils tuned to the harmonies of a multi-dimensional season.

In lowland meadows farmers have taken their first hay crop and are already studying the ears of corn now growing fat in neighbouring fields, making their tentative forecasts for the coming grain harvest. It's a time of promise, of hope made good and anticipation for tomorrow. But while June sun bathes the low-lying meadows with its benediction, in the mountains of the High Pyrénées winter still holds the uppermost slopes in its grip, and summer must wait its turn.

The overnight train from Paris delivered us to Luchon in time for breakfast. As ever there were clouds hanging low over the mountains: our usual greeting. The boulevard was wet with overnight rain, dark and shining, but as we drank our coffee and ate croissants we could feel the warmth of the morning sun working to our advantage, and soon the streets were steaming. What, I wondered, would be the condition of the mountains? For now we could only speculate, as they were hidden from view by the clouds. Dense forests rose steeply out of the valley on the edge of town to be swallowed by an overall grey scum that stretched from one limited horizon to another.

Through that scum the sun's warmth penetrated, but not its light. Luchon's beret sat tight.

When first we started to visit these mountains we were innocent enough to spend an initial couple of hours or so walking the road that leads out of town towards the frontier peaks. Not so now. We called a taxi, dumped the over-heavy rucksacks into the boot of the Citroen, and travelled in style. Reality would descend upon us soon enough, but I'd much rather that be experienced with spongy turf or the rock of the mountains beneath my boots, than tarmac. So we sat in deep-cushioned comfort and drove past orchards flush with blossom, and meadows where blue-smocked peasants made hay with

_____

Early morning among the pines in Valhiverna (Kev Reynolds).

long-handled scythes, reminding me of days in the Alps and Constable prints of old-time England — an England long given over to machinery, while here in the mountains traditional ways lived on.

Beyond the orchards came forest. Dense forest. A deep green blanket of conifers, mature, stately, dark in its interior, safely containing the steep mountain wall in a cover that stretched from valley floor to cloud ceiling. Through that forest ran streams. Along its edge grew wild raspberries that I knew well from September visits but for now only a few wood anemones made a half-hearted display of colour. All else was green.

Then came reality at last. The road ran out. Ahead the valley curved to the right, and out of sight it was closed off by linking ridges of unseen peaks. There were no more forests, just a spinney or two of pines and the hillsides rising all round us. Here the clouds were higher, but we could look back down-valley towards the forest and see how the trees drew vapour to them, jealously holding on to their own personal climate. Ours was dictated by the mountains whose upper slopes we still could not see, but below the clouds were snow-tails that told enough about the progress—or lack of it—of summer up there, in the clouds. Winter was evidently still in command.

Our route lay away from the main valley. A wooden bridge took us over the stream and a broad path led on. Familiar from previous trips we recognized individual boulders and the occasional tree, acknowledged the giant of a shepherd who leaned dreamily on his stick, a small rucksack on his back with an umbrella projecting from it, and did not realize that he would be the last human being we'd see for about ten days. His sheep grazed as they walked, quite unconcerned by our passage among them, and it was only the alert head-pricking of the shepherd's dog that gave any illusion of liveliness to the scene. Time had no real meaning. The shepherd's way of life had little in it, other than the slow evolution of the seasons, to distinguish one day from another. We were merely figures in a clouded landscape; as indeed he was to us.

It wasn't long before we were knee-deep in snow and the path was lost to us. We knew the way, though, from previous years, and took out ice-axes to probe the upward route. Mountains rose sharply in a constricting

Among the clouds on the Val de Joeu (Kev Reynolds).

narrow-walled hanging valley. Mist played about in the dark recesses of couloirs and tore itself among the crags. We had traded trees and grass for snow and ice and rock; summer for winter. And this, I told myself, was the same June that lit the meadows at home. Above these clouds the same sun beamed that was beaming through beechwoods in Kent and Surrey. Here it loosened snow and sent stones clattering down gullies, while at home and in the valley below it set the grasses seething with insect life. Midsummer, according to the calendar, was but a couple of weeks away. Slugging through snowfields at only 8,000 ft, I found that difficult to believe.

A few hundred feet below the nick of a pass that would take us over into Spain, there lies a bowl of mountain containing within it a handful of tarns. During summer it is a pleasant place, just right for a picnic. There are flowers along the shores of the tarns and fine views out towards the foothills of France. Behind the lakes mountains curve in an attractive little cirque; they rise from anklets of scree in great buttresses and slabs to the ridge along which runs the international border. In summer a path zig-zags tightly above the screes, twists

round a buttress and climbs in shadow to the pass itself. But now all was lost in a swirl of cloud and snow. And what was worse, the warmth of mid-day made that snow extremely unstable. To attempt to reach the pass now would be to risk avalanche. There was nothing for it but to spend the night here and make an early start in the morning when the snow and ice would still be gripped by frost.

There's a hut beside one of the tarns. A small, single-roomed affair with a low roof, one window, a fireplace and sleeping platform capable of holding perhaps ten people — so long as they're good friends. We had it to ourselves, as we had on previous occasions too. In this hut we'd spent several cold and uncomfortable nights while bad weather roared outside. Sometimes the only way in was through the window, for the door would be blocked by snowdrifts. Often snow had come down the chimney and even now was spilling across the floor from the fireplace in billows of ice. On one occasion we had even cowered within the hut as an avalanche flowed over the roof. It was certainly no palace, but by offering the opportunity to cross safely into Spain in the morning, it was adequate and acceptable.

During the long hours of our internment I thought of other Junes in these, and other mountains elsewhere. I thought of the Alps and the valley in Switzerland that had been my home for a couple of years, where June was a dirty month to begin with, scruffy with old snowbanks melting across the meadows, to be replaced by drifts of alpine flowers that took your breath away. I remembered walks in neighbouring valleys, bright beneath the sun that had brought summer several weeks earlier than in the valley of my home, which was higher and subject to other influences.

My mind dwelt too on numerous June visits to the Pyrénées, a range I had first discovered in such a month of transition as this was to be. Then, on that first visit, I had learned how carefully the visitor must walk, for I had attempted to cross into Spain by way of the Brèche de Roland — that huge gash in the wall of the Cirque de Gavarnie formed when a delicately eroded block of mountain as high as

Sera del Neres holds on to the last vestige of spring (Kev Reynolds).

a church toppled into the arid wilderness above Ordesa long before Charlemagne's retreat from the Moor. On my way to it a snow bridge gave way beneath my weight and I had plunged through into an unseen stream; icy, fast-flowing and unwelcome. Above that the slopes were treacherous beyond words. They were poised for avalanche and I had turned back wet and disconsolate, but safe.

On another occasion I strolled in the Marcadau Valley with my family, through meadows blue-flecked with gentians, then climbed higher in the hope of making a circuit of a region of lost tarns and waterfalls that we felt would be seen at their very best in June. It was a steep walk among trees and over streams, climbing into a hanging valley where, alas, at the very first tarn, icebergs were floating as in an arctic scene, and it became obvious that above it there could be no safe continuation of our walk. The scars of recent avalanche were there for all to see; nature advertising without subtlety the dangers to be met by the impetuous and foolhardy. Again, retreat was in order, but in the valley itself there were consolations to be found in the foaming streams and flowers that adorned rock face and pasture, and at the head of the valley, where it broadens to a fan of great beauty, there were izard — the chamois of the Pyrénées — grazing nearby below the snowfields that would soon be melting up the hillsides.

A few days later we were in the Rioumajou, that green bowl of luxury, warm in the sun that spoke of full summer. There were cattle standing knee-deep in the river to cool themselves, and sheep huddled together in the shade of a clump of pine trees on a hillock. High above the heights were out of bounds. Up there it was still full winter. But we were content to wander the woods and meadows, leaping streams, bathing in a secluded pool, delighting to the variety of flowers and shrubs coming into bloom and watching as the breeze caught among the pines and wafted clouds of yellow pollen across the valley. Our valley stood calm in the benevolence of midsummer and the air was full of fragrance.

I felt certain, as I lay through the hours of darkness in the snow-bound hut, that beyond the ridge the Esera Valley would be ready to receive summer. While here in this French cirque winter had some days yet to run, over in Spain the sun would have been at work.

The Esera valley in transition from winter to summer (Kev Reynolds).

Over there we would find again flowers and streams and green turf pastures. Over there, in the valley bed, a season of colour and life and fragrance would be waiting. First, though, we must shrug off the manacles of winter.

Each valley addresses summer in its own fashion, depending upon the peculiarities of altitude, direction of slope or position in relation to its walling mountains, and the influence of air streams. In some valleys, experience told me, summer will be colouring south-facing hillsides while but a few hundred yards away, facing north, winter snows still lie almost to the valley floor. Avalanches come roaring from exposed heights, clearing in one fell swoop the upper slopes, while in others that snow will remain throughout the year. In one valley it is possible to experience two contrasting seasons merely by walking from one side to the other.

Elsewhere in the Pyrénées it is the flowers that call the seasons. The flower garden of

become intoxicated by their fragrance. There are times when the Vall d'Aran and Cerdagne, for example, appear from a distance to be carpeted with drifts of snow, but on closer inspection that snow turns out to be a profusion of narcissi; swamp upon swamp of them, heady with their scent, the warm air of early summer wrapping the valleys in perfume.

It was the thought of the Esera in bloom, just beyond the steep rise of mountains outside the hut, that fuelled my anticipation of it. Morning was a long time coming, and then when it did, it was hard with frost. Outside the snow was crunchy under foot, and a clear sky high overhead gave promise for the day. We had only a short distance to travel, but it was essential that we went early, before the sun could penetrate this icy bowl. So we strapped crampons to our boots, gripped ice-axes in gloved hands, and set off for the hidden pass beyond which lay summer.

In shadow, on ice, we crunched upward, skirting the base of the verglassed crags in a rising traverse above slopes that plunged to the still ice-bound tarns. Round the buttress, then steeply up towards a sharp 'V' of sunlight in a tight cleft that told of the pass. The slope grew steeper, the walls on either side increasingly constricted. Beneath the snow and ice I knew there was a twisting path where, for centuries, muleteers carried out a trade from one side of the mountains to the other, and where even armies had marched in the long-ago days when France and Spain were sworn enemies. Now only folk memories remained, and the firm knowledge that within a couple of weeks or so that path would again be obvious and inviting to other walkers and climbers. Today we made our own trail, panting towards the sun.

The pass gained, we looked out with relief and sheer pleasure at the mountains rising majestically across the valley; at those familiar peaks jutting above the Escaleta to the east; at glaciers and snowfields and high ridges gleaming in the brilliant dazzle of a June morning. Spain. Not the Spain of high-rise hotels and kiss-me-quick hats, nor that of bullfights and castanets and guitars in the moonlight; but a Spain of lost-world magnificence. Big mountains, lush valleys, booming cascades, little tarns and streams and glorious flower meadows and a fragrance peculiar to valleys in the heart of the Spanish Pyrénées. In that breath of early summer came a taste of Africa mingling with snow and ice

Europe. There are so many different influences at work here to make it so; different rock types, different climatic pressures, different regions whose native flora has spread into the mountains. There are flowers straying here that are normally associated with low-lying areas far north of the Pyrénées, mingling with those generally seen along the Mediterranean. There are alpine species familiar from other mountain regions, and more than a hundred distinct types unique to the Pyrénées. It's not necessary to have a knowledge of botany to be aware of the richness of this flora, and wandering among these valleys in June is to

June in the Pyrenees: the early morning view east from the Aneto Glacier (Kev Reynolds).

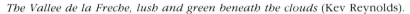

The Vallee de la Freche, lush and green beneath the clouds (Kev Reynolds).

High in the Pyrenees, above Vallee de la Freche, the snow is old and granular (Kev Reynolds).

and crystal streams. There was promise in the view and in the breeze. We had emerged from the shadows to find ourselves now bathed in sunlight. Behind was winter. Ahead lay a mixture of seasons. We were to experience all but autumn within a few days.

Down we went stepping through acres of pleasure, across snow slopes through which tufts of early grass sprouted, over iced pools and along terraces where snow still lay banked in drifts from the long months of hoary cold. As our descent took us lower towards the valley floor, so the snow became more shallow, patchy, melting at the edges. As it did, up came the scent of damp turf under foot. Streamlets trickled through the grass and down the path, joining forces where they'd been funnelled by a fold of hillside, they grew to streams with body that gurgled as they flowed, then poured in silvery cascades over rocks and boulders jutting from the slope. There were fat salamanders, orange and black coated, waddling as though on sore feet across our path. Ugly creatures, they were, but quite

harmless. Later we would see numerous lizards, but, cautious creatures, the day was not yet warm enough for them to lay out sunning themselves.

Below the last patch of snow, on a hillside terrace with magnificent views down-valley to the peaks of Literole, we pitched the tent. It was a hillside camp of rare perfection. Behind the tent ran a clear stream destined to be the water supply for the duration of our stay. There was a flat-topped rock midstream where I could sit to draw a billy of water for cooking purposes, and where I would wash-up afterwards. From it I had a glimpse through a brief defile to the next valley level below, the view framed by juniper on one side and a clump of alpenroses on the other. On occasion I would gaze directly onto an izard who came down from the upper slopes to drink from our stream. A little farther up-valley shrill whistles from a jumble of rocks revealed where a colony of marmots lived. Their anxious calls became a daily background to which we soon grew accustomed.

But best of all were the flowers that appeared all around the tent during the next few days. There were trumpet gentians and primulas and two different orchids, and a pattern of dogstooth violets, their tassled heads looking a little like those of fuchsias as they swung to and fro in the breeze. There were several clumps of alpenroses forming a natural boundary to our site. When we arrived they were bare of bloom, but as the days progressed and the sun worked its wizardry, so blooms unfurled, and by the time we left the valley we could look down from a high ridge or a solitary peak we had spent several hours climbing, and detect our camp by the blazing red of our neighbourhood shrubbery. Then there were the dwarf pines whose scent filled our heads from the first day to the last, and the juniper sprays that gave off a fragrance not unlike blackcurrants when we brushed against them. The scent of summer was in the air at last.

Keith, who was with me, is a camper with many bright ideas, and he soon scouted among the pines for branches or tufts of greenery that had been stripped by winter snow or avalanche. Returning with arms full of his bounty he set about spreading a mattress beneath the groundsheet, and as a result the tent became filled with its resinous perfume, and there we enjoyed nights of great comfort on our springy pine bed. Pine tufts were also adopted as a weapon in the fight to keep mosquitoes at bay. Towards evening when the evil insects came flying in search of flesh, Keith would create a tripod of tent pegs from which he strung a tuft of pine. Beneath it he fixed a stub of candle so that the flame from it barely touched the pine, but rather gently singed it. The mosquitoes would not fly through the wisp of smoke at the tent's entrance, and thus saved from their attentions we also had the additional fragrance of pine-smoke within the tent.

From the doorway of the tent our view encompassed first the terrace of flowers, then the shrubs and dwarf pine, then off to the slopes of the Maladeta massif. Up and up our eyes were drawn to hanging valleys filled with snow, and beyond them to the glaciers, dying now, yet whose past centuries of industry had been responsible for creating the idyll that was today's Esera Valley. And above the glaciers the granite spine containing peaks upon which I had spent so many days of activity in

previous years and, God willing, would do so again. Peaks like that of Maladeta itself and its superb western arète in whose tiny crevices I had discovered with breathless surprise magnificent minute flowers, cushion plants on ledges, and rocks splashed with artists' palettes of lichens. No-one could accuse the Maladeta of being a dead, lifeless mountain. Only the foolish and ignorant would jump to such conclusions, for we who had scrambled upon its ridges and walked in its shadow with our eyes open, knew the truth.

In that big, broad massif were glacial corries hiding little tarns around which I knew were

The last part of the Esera to take on summer is the High Valleta de la Escaleta (Kev Reynolds).

numerous flowery patches. And nature herself had been instrumental in creating a garden from the genesis-like wilderness of its ancient moraines. Gone was the ice now. At first glance a grey desert of rock and scree and grit remained, yet among that world of apparent lifelessness, shrubs and flowers grew in abundance, and I wondered how many more years it would take before high meadows cushioned those rocks. How long before sheep would be grazing where today's moraine banks

were slowly being adopted by individual plants and the first pioneer grasses?

Being June, with summer still but a promise away on the peaks, there was still a great deal of snow. In a month or so all this would appear so different. I had been here in the Esera to walk and climb in September. I'd wandered through, crossing high passes at either end of the valley when summer had played its full hand, and found a very different landscape. Then the glaciers were dry — that is

Wild camping among the pines in the Esera valley (Kev Reynolds).

Top right July: *Looking west from Sgurr nan Coireachan with the flat-topped island of Eigg slightly to the left before the hills of Rum in the middle distance* (Roger Smith).

Bottom right July: *Looking south-east from Gairich towards the distant Ben Nevis, standing well clear of the clouds and slightly to the right of centre on the far skyline* (Roger Smith).

to say, bare of snow. They appeared somewhat drab, dirty, shrunken excuses for past glories. Certainly they gave shorter routes to climb, for there was no wallowing through deep soft snow, and the rock was warm to the touch, dry and clean to scramble on. Today it would be ice-veneered, some of it definitely out of bounds. In September the alpenroses in the valley had finished with bloom, and only crinkled rust-coloured seed-pods told of their former flourish. There would be no orchids or dogstooth violets, but instead great splashes of autumn crocus where now our tent stood. Every season has its special attributes, and if you love the mountains, not just for themselves, but for all their many facets, you'll never be disappointed.

But there's nothing quite like June. Then there's a distinct crispness in the air, the toothpaste-fresh nip of early morning when frost still holds the grasses and flowers brittle in its grasp. Later, comes the sun: a brilliance that pours from clear skies radiant beams, dazzling on snowfield, glacier, stream and tarn

alike — working on the hillsides, beating back all trace of winter and inspiring transient spring. Hillsides freed suddenly from their burden of snow, sport springy turf, out of which, hour by glorious hour, new flowers emerge where there had been no flowers before. Daily we witnessed this transformation. We'd leave the tent in the early morning bound for a climb or a walk of exploration, and return later in the day to find winter had receded farther and farther up the hillside.

One day we set out on a climb along the frontier ridge. Halfway up our hillside approach we came upon a shallow tarn trapped on a terraced ledge. A lovely glistening pearl of a tarn, it was, turning neighbourhood mountains on their heads. Around its edge frogs belched in the morning sunlight. When we'd come down this way on our arrival in the valley, we must have walked across it over snow and ice without knowing of its existence. Yet when we returned at the end of our sojourn, it had gone; evaporated in the bright June sun, only a tide-mark reminder in the

Above August: *This view of the Llangattock escapement from the east demonstrates its dramatic impact upon the South Wales landscape* (Kevin Walker).

Above right August: *The limestone summit of Pen Cerrigcalch gleams in the sunlight of an August noon beyond the unquarried limestone pinnacle known as the 'Lonely Shepherd'* (Kevin Walker).

Right August: *The black mountains as viewed from Mynydd Clandadoch near Crickhowell, South Wales* (Kevin Walker).

Above August: *The view from the lower tram road on Clandadoch. The Black Mountains rise in afternoon sunlight from the pastoral Usk valley* (Kevin Walker).

Below September: *By September the sycamores in the Trossachs have begun to turn* (Jim Crumley).

Below September: *This month also brings out the best colour in the Loch Laggan Rowan. Here a small specimen struggles to make its presence felt between the rocks* (Jim Crumley).

Right September: *The River Snizort forms a silver link with its headwaters in the Cuillin mountains beyond* (Jim Crumley).

Below September: *The view north over Loch Katrine to the Crianlarich hills from high on Ben Venue* (Jim Crumley).

grass bearing witness to its being. In those two weeks we had experienced the full evolution from winter, through spring and into summer on the slopes of the mountain.

Our climbs were often repetitions of routes we'd enjoyed in previous years; sometimes new ways on familiar mountains, sometimes fresh peaks that we discovered for ourselves. Every one was worth spending time on. There were butterflies drifting over the ridges, and even ants in residence on a summit at 10,000 ft. There were huge vistas within whose compass there was nothing made by man, and we gazed for long periods in complete satisfaction at far-off mountains we had climbed in other years, in other seasons. How comforting it was to be out here and to know so many individual summits guarding distant valleys. Knowing specific features of those unseen valleys, remembering their particular glories, their lakes, pastures, rock faces and passes. It was a beautiful world, lit by that life-giving sun that was every minute playing creator to landscapes in the midst of development and revolution. From snow patch to flower garden. The gift of June in the High Pyrénées.

Marmots had emerged from hibernation.

We'd see them sometimes, ruffled and a little dozy from their long slumber underground. They'd play and feed and romp across the grass. They'd suddenly sit bolt upright, noses twitching, eyes peering ahead for sign of danger. There'd be a shrill whistle and away they'd go, plunging underground again for safety. They were our neighbours in the Esera: they and the izard, and the salamanders, and lizards; and the frogs that took charge of a pool a hundred yards away upstream; and the finches twittering and flitting from one pine perch to another. Then there were the butterflies that rose in drifts of blue from the swampy ground lower in the valley where fifty years ago there had been a tarn or two — a boggy stretch rich in flowers and cotton grass.

In the Valleta de la Escaleta, the eastern extension of the Esera's upper sanctuary, at the head of which stands the double-prolonged Forcanada, spring was reluctant to intrude. It's a high valley, is the Escaleta. A high turmoil of pits and pools and cascades. Underground are several potholes explored decades ago by the great Norbert Casteret; in June they were disguised beneath a deep coverlet of snow and it was necessary to tread with caution. The peaks were dressed still in winter garb, the

A sure sign of summer in the Pyrenees: snow-melt enlivens streams in the Pomero valley (Kev Reynolds).

valley itself uncertain of the date. But beyond that the Vall del Joeu, 2,000 ft lower than the Escaleta, had summer wrapped in its embrace. Not a sign of snow down there in the valley, but green meadows, green trees, clear pools and streams and flowers in abundance. It was warm, too.

Cutting west of the Vall del Joeu, and linked to the Esera by the saddle of Port de la Picada, lies the Pomero Valley. That too was a delight in June. Fragrant pools of colour accompanied every step as we climbed through it. Bilberries and alpenroses tangled together. Then daffodils and narcissi, and orchids — the elder-flowered

orchid here in considerable numbers — and gentians. Then a patch of velvet-headed fritillaries mixed among cowslips and oxlips. Higher still a magnificent little bush of daphne mezereum wearing a halo of perfume, so powerful that we were aware of it even before we saw it, and whose fragrance remained long after we had continued on our way.

The Port de la Picada was deep still in snow, but before we traded once again grass slopes for winter, we discovered a scattering of dogstooth violets below the Col de l'Infern and, among the rocks, a few lovely spring anemones just opening their fried-egg coloured

Right *Flower-splashed hillsides leading to Port de Venasque* (Kev Reynolds).

Above right *Winter is reluctant to leave the Escaleta* (Kev Reynolds).

flowers to the sun. Then back into winter until the pass was crossed and we could descend once more to our tent in the Esera.

We deserted the valley on another occasion when we climbed Aneto and descended south in the face of a storm, glissading fast down the Glacier de Coronas with lightning fizzing about us; down to tarns and boulder slopes and eventually forest cover, which in turn brought us to a hut in the upper reaches of the Vallhiverna. It was raining hard and we were soaked. Around the hut were several pine trees brought down during the winter. We dragged a slender one into the hut, stuffed one end into the fireplace and gave ourselves warmth. Throughout the night we lay beside the fire, and whenever one of us awoke with cold, the tree would be pushed deeper into the fireplace where it would burst into flame and bring instant warmth again.

Next day all trace of storm had passed and the full brilliance of a Spanish summer was burning the sky. We wandered down-valley with hearts high. There were flowers in the meadows again, and the Pyrénéan endemic, *Ramonda myconi*, brilliant within the rock face that bordered the track that took us back down into the lower levels of the Esera. There we turned north and headed back to the sanctuary; back to our tent on its hillside terrace. Back to the marmots, izard, butterflies and salamanders and our own personal garden of flowers. Ours, at least, for this short spell. Ours in memory today, for the magic of June in the High Pyrénées is a transient spectacle that we always treasure and hope to encounter again.

Next Year

Kev Reynolds worked for nearly twenty years as a Youth Hostel Warden, but is now a freelance writer, photographer and lecturer specializing in countryside and mountain topics. A frequent contributor to outdoor magazines, he has walked and climbed in most of the high mountain areas of Europe and North Africa. He is the author of several guide books for walkers, including one on the Pyrénées.

The endless daylight of July

ROGER SMITH

As Peter and I walked up the glen in the long summer gloaming, the hills that were our target for the morrow turned black against the slowly darkening sky. We walked in peace, the soft night air around us almost palpable. By the time we reached the bothy, it was almost midnight but there was just enough light for us to see our way in and to find to our pleasure that the place was equipped with mattresses on which we could lay our sleeping bags.

A last brew of tea, drunk standing in the doorway so as to absorb all the feeling of the summer night, and we turned in. Within four hours it would be light again, the start, we hoped, of a long, fulfilling mountain day. As I drifted off to sleep, my thoughts turned back nearly forty years to a scene of my childhood.

July has always meant for me a time of release, a time when the days seemed almost endless and play was paramount. I was raised in London, and once I had reached an age where I was allowed out on my own, summer memories are of open spaces, deep woods and the discovery of 'secret' and (to us) enchanted hollows, often supplied with ponds teeming with wildlife. All this was to be found only a modest bus ride from home, on the expanse of Wimbledon Common.

I didn't realize until many years later how much it had meant to me: it was a place I took very much for granted, a place that would always be there for long summer days. Inasmuch as that was possible in our ordered city lives, my pals and I had total freedom up on the common, and we took full advantage of it. I can vividly remember lying back on a grassy bank and listening to a skylark singing, trying to spot the tiny scrap of bones and feathers making this incredible sound against the hot sun — and failing.

It seems now, looking back on those July days of the late 1940s and early 1950s, that there always was hot sun. I don't recall being up on the Common walking in the rain, though doubtless we were. Once school broke up for the long vacation, summer stretched

ahead of us forever, and it seemed it would always be July and always the sun would be shining on the birchy glades and wide heathland of Wimbledon Common. Although I could not realize it at the time, my subsequent love of wild country, especially mountains, and my innate and inextinguishable passion for the conservation of such places must have been born in those summer days of my later childhood. The freedom that we enjoyed then was a thing beyond price, and I have tried to pass on some of that to my own children. Time will tell if I have succeeded.

My adult, and working, life matured towards mountains only slowly, but eventually in the mid-1970s I came to Scotland to live and work (as editor of *The Great Outdoors*) and found myself in the hills more and more frequently. My love of the wild places deepened, nurtured both by my own experiences and by my considerable good fortune in finding hill companions who felt as I did and who taught me hillcraft and respect for the mountains and their often savage weather — yes, even in July!

Although I have for many years gone out in all seasons and all weather I feel no shame in admitting that the spring and summer are the times I like the best in Scotland. Winter has its own beauty but it is a season of cruelty too, an unforgiving time when you must always be on your guard. I have enjoyed deeply rewarding expeditions in winter, but the enjoyment has come from conquering the conditions and my own frailties rather than from the mountains themselves.

The real hill year begins for me in May — in some years perhaps in April — with the rapidly lengthening days and the disappearance of the snow. I have walked across Scotland three times in May, and I have taken a number of fine hill-based holidays, both with and without my family, in June and July. In those midsummer weeks the days are of such lengths as to expand the ambitions to almost infinite horizons: even if you are benighted it is generally warm enough to simply sleep out for those few hours when the light is chasing round the northern rim of the world towards the start of another day.

It may not always be so, of course. I have stood on the summit of Bynack Mor in July, having navigated my way up there through thick mist, and watched a heavy snow shower drift across Strath Nethy from the invisible summit of Cairngorm a couple of miles away. On that day I needed the hat and gloves that are *always* in my pack regardless of the time of year or the weather forecast. But more often than not there is a time in July when one of those lovely oval areas of high pressure drifts up to us from the continent or the Azores and even in the Scottish Highland we enjoy magnificent days of unbroken warm sunshine. In those days I glory to the very fibre of my being for the infinite joy of just having hills to walk and wild wide spaces to traverse in freedom. Such a time was before Peter and I as we left our bothy shelter.

The bothy was Corryhully in Glen Finnan.

The previous evening, the last train from Fort William had dropped us at Glenfinnan Station with enough time for a pint at the Stage House Inn before our late night wander up the glen to our resting place. Bothying is an art pretty well peculiar to the Scottish Highlands and is something I have greatly come to enjoy. These simple unlocked shelters are available for genuine travellers for most of the year: many of them are maintained through the voluntary efforts of the Mountain Bothies Association. Corryhully is an exception. It is kept by the Glenfinnan Estate but bears a notice on its door welcoming responsible walkers and asking them to leave it in good condition for those who follow.

That we did early on a bright and already warm Saturday morning as we shut the door behind us and headed towards Sgurr nan Coireachan, our first Munro of the day. The pursuit of these 277 summits over 3,000 ft is a game I've been happily playing for a good few years now (along with many others!). I've not

The unusual 'tor' of the Barns of Bynack — Bynack Mor — Cairngorms (Hamish Brown).

Above *Corryhully bothy, in Glen Finnan* (Roger Smith).

Right *Peter Evans at the summit of Sgurr nan Coireachan, above Glen Finnan, looking north* (Roger Smith).

Above right *A geometric 'choke' of conifers — view down into Glendoll* (Hamish Brown).

too many left to climb, and in amassing the full list I will have traversed much of the very finest of Scotland's scenery. That was certainly true of the trip that started in Glen Finnan.

We were on Ordnance Survey 1:50,000 sheet 40. North of the point where we left the railway is an area of 400 square kilometres with no roads and only two permanently occupied dwellings. It is mountain country *par excellence,* yet there is an inherent sadness about it too. It is empty largely because the people who formerly lived there and worked the land were cleared off in the 18th and early 19th centuries: sent to the colonies to make way for sheep, which were judged to be more profitable, and for deer stalking.

Now there is another clearance. How ever much I love the hills — and I am not poet enough to express that love adequately in words — I can never wander such places without feeling regret at their emptiness of the people who should live and work here. In July all these West Highland glens ought to be populated by folk using the 'shielings' — the summer dwellings on the higher ground — to tend and cultivate their stock and crops. They have gone and I fear will never return, especially as so many of these glens are now being buried under the smothering blanket of commercial conifer forestry. It was so in every glen we traversed on that trip, without exception.

We had started early and the intensity of

daylight in July in the Scottish Highlands meant that there was no pressure of time on us whatsoever. That is a wonderful feeling. We were totally free to go as long or as short a distance as we wanted in the day. As it turned out, we needed that adaptability throughout our time in the hills. By nine o'clock we were on the ridge of Sgurr a'Choire Riabhaich, Coireachan's southern outlier. The sun was high and hot and the ground underfoot was rough and broken so our pace was of necessity somewhat measured. But what did it matter? The day and the hills were ours to enjoy and just as in winter it is ever important to keep on the right side of hypothermia so on these rare full summer days it saves much anguish if the body temperature is kept below boiling point.

The summit of Sgurr nan Coireachan with its OS triangulation pillar was a viewpoint of some magnificence. Hills, glens and lochs baked and shimmered under the glowing sun. We gloried in it all. To the west especially was splendour and richness, that happy combination of water and upthrust land that sets Scotland apart from anywhere else I know. I have puzzled long over what it is that makes these West Highland scenes so majestic and I can only think it must be the perfection of scale. Nothing is too high or too deep: it all fits together beautifully, and the celestial architect responsible must be well satisfied with this particular corner of his world.

Right *The classic view of Glenfinnan looking down Loch Shiel with the monument to the forty five in the foreground* (Hamish Brown).

Below *The monument to the forty five — seen from Loch Shiel* (Hamish Brown).

Below right *From the foot of Glen Dessarry — looking to the Streaps and Sgurr Thuilm* (Hamish Brown).

Having drunk copiously of that cup of western magic, it was somehow fitting to turn east to continue our journey. Now we had a fine high level promenade over two intervening tops to our second Munro, Sgurr Thuilm. Among those who had traversed this peak before us was none other than Prince Charles Edward Stuart, during that desperate summer of 1746 when he ran as a fugitive through Highland Scotland, being passed unseen from one small band of sympathisers to another. His wild and ultimately sad story is well told at the National Trust for Scotland visitor centre in Glenfinnan.

Nobody was chasing us, which was just as well. The ridge we were traversing, fine though it was, held any number of small interruptions in outcrops and rock dykes, and our pace slowed still further. On the final pull up to the summit of Sgurr Thuilm we met another couple, the only people we were to encounter on the whole three-day walk. Empty lands indeed: and the worse for it.

Topping Sgurr Thuilm brought a sense of achievement and, strangely, relief. No more hills to be climbed today: we could enjoy an afternoon of leisure in the glorious hot sunshine, wandering down the hill and through Glen Pean to go back up Glen Dessarry a little way to our second bothy. Indolence grasped us very rapidly, and shortly below Sgurr Thuilm's rocky top we spent quite a while, on the pretext of 'route planning', discussing exactly where we would stop for lunch. As if it mattered! One of the great delights of summer hillwalking is the time you spend doing nothing, and we enjoyed just such a time now beside the Allt a Choire Dhuibh. The Gaelic name means 'burn of the black corrie' but nothing could have been less black than our situation. We lazed beside the chuckling water, brewed up and drank tea, and actually had to cover up against the now quite fierce sun — not a common occurrence in the Highlands!

An hour passed very agreeably. During that time we agreed to make for A'Chuil bothy in Glen Dessarry, which would leave us well placed for tomorrow's hills. There had been a thought that we might try to get further round,

to Sourlies on Loch Nevis, but that would have meant a long slog late into the evening — and besides, on such a magnificent weekend it was likely that Sourlies would be crowded with folk 'doing' the Knoydart hills.

So we wandered happily down to Glen Pean and along the glen towards Strathan, the steading placed where Pean and Dessarry meet, at the west end of Loch Arkaig. There are many people who have looked forward to walking the length of Loch Arkaig as part of a through trek and have been sore disappointed to find that the dozen miles of road on the loch's northern shore are tarmaced all the way. It's still a lovely walk, but hard on the feet forbye!

We were sorry to find the area immediately west of Strathan a bit of a tangle, with young forestry and numerous tracks not marked on our map, and were glad to extricate ourselves from it and head back west up Glen Dessarry, into the late afternoon sun. There is much forestry here too, with service tracks extending far up the glen. Such planting has attracted a great deal of criticism in recent times, with some justification, I believe. It is the *system* which is wrong, encouraging as it does the planting of large blocks of even-aged conifers of only one or two unattractive species. I believe there is a

great deal of scope in Scotland for better forestry, including a lot more hardwoods and native pine, but that is a subject I had better not discourse on here or we will never get back to our summer walk!

We allowed the magnificence of the mountain scenery to compensate for the blight of the forestry and we gazed in some awe at the wall of hills soaring up above the north side of the glen. Tomorrow morning we would have to climb that lot, and if the heatwave continued it would be a fair hike. But no matter. For the time being we would concentrate on reaching A'Chuil, settling in, and enjoying a lazy bothy evening. In wet weather the River Dessarry can be very difficult to cross but there were to be no such problems today. After passing Upper Glendessarry, which was occupied, presumably by folk up for the weekend, we cut down to the river, hopped across on boulders with ease, and made our way up to the bothy. It is snugly set against the hill but the forestry is all around it and when the trees are grown it will alas be somewhat buried.

We wondered how many people would be there. On such a weekend, in such an area, it was almost inconceivable that we should have

Left *The other Sgurr nan Coirea-chan from the forestry track in Glen Dessarry* (Roger Smith).

Below left *Strathan, at the west end of Loch Arkaig and at the point where Glen Dessarry and Glen Pean meet* (Roger Smith).

the place to ourselves, but that is just what happened. Maybe they were all at Sourlies! A'Chuil is a fine bothy and we enjoyed our night there greatly. After making our supper and eating it we took our coffee outside and tried to work out the best way of breaching the wall facing us to reach the ridge. Ambitious plans laid before the trip had included Sgurr na Ciche and Garbh Choich Mor but we decided that might be asking too much. We would therefore head for Sgurr nan Coireachan and see how we felt from there.

I can seen confusion arising in the mind of the reader here. Yes, it's the same name as one of the Glen Finnan hills. This is not at all uncommon in Scotland (or anywhere else where there are hills, for that matter). The names were bestowed by people in the glens looking up and if 'peak of the corries' (as in this case) or 'grey hill' or 'speckled hill' seemed an appropriate name, what matter if there might be another hill so named miles away on somebody else's land?

There seemed from the map to be a deep

glen leading up the ridge a little way east of Coireachan. If it went, it would perhaps be a feasible way up without having to tackle the unremitting slopes of the hill itself. We would see in the morning. For now we were content to settle down into our sleeping bags for the night. The 'bothy book' at A'Chuil, as indeed at Corryhully, had warned of a resident mouse, but they must have both been away on holiday, for in each case we slept undisturbed.

The Sunday morning was every bit as splendid as Saturday's had been. Underfoot it started none too well for us. The forest road behind the bothy proved too much of a temptation and we stayed with it too far to the west, having to cut across through rough young plantations to cross the river and reach the path on the north side of the glen — a great through route to Knoydart and the west coast.

We left the path to traverse a shoulder of hill into the glen of the Allt Coire nan Uth (possibly 'corrie of the udders' indicating a

Right *Peter Evans on the scramble up the dry burn towards Sgurr nan Coireachan* (Roger Smith).

Below *Sgurr na Ciche and the Knoydart hills from Sgurr nan Coireachan above Glen Dessarry* (Roger Smith).

Below right *Sgurr Mor — seen from the north* (Hamish Brown).

place where cattle might be taken in summer). As we came over the shoulder we could see to our relief that the glen would provide a good way up to the ridge. In fact it was a very fine way up. In the higher reaches the burn tumbled over several small falls, and with the water as low as it was in that hot spell, there was fun to be had scrambling up the rocks and slabs. A high lochan nestled under the ridge was an irresistible brew spot. We could already sense that our decision not to head further west was a wise one. It was *hot*, as it rarely is — not merely warm but intensely hot, and walking with a pack in such conditions on the type of rough ground we were traversing was damned hard work.

The compensations came as soon as we reached the ridge. The views in every direction were magnificent. To the west, the Knoydart hills and the Inner Hebrides sweeping round from Eigg to Skye. To the north the serried ranks of the Kintail hills and beyond them more and more peaks. To the east the Lochaber giants with Nevis as always humped above them in unmistakable profile.

This was great, especially as we could leave our packs at the point where we gained the ridge and scramble up to the summit of Sgurr nan Coireachan unladen. We were in the centre of a quite superb stretch of mountains

and our cameras were kept very busy for the next few minutes. Capturing the scene on film is a poor substitute for experience of the real thing but when confronted with such splendour it is no wonder that we try. The twin rough humps of Sgurr na Ciche and Garbh Choich Mor tempted us, briefly, but to reach them and return would have taken a heavy toll. They won't go away and in any case deserve a full day to themselves. Our day went east, and we were careful to cover our necks to avoid the risk of sunburn. We had also filled our water carrier by the lochan before gaining the ridge — a long traverse without water would be no joke.

The first objective was to traverse An Eag ('the notch') to reach the twin tops of Sgurr Beag and then Sgurr Mor (simply, in order, 'little' and 'big peak'), the latter being a Munro. From the map I could see that the ridge was pathed from Sgurr Beag onwards. This would undoubtedly be a stalking path, constructed in late Victorian or Edwardian times in the heyday of the great sporting estates. These paths had to carry ponies and provisions to the high stalking grounds and they were made with great care and skill. Those that are left in reasonable condition are an immense help to the hill walker of today. They invariably climb hills by the easiest way up, taking many zig-

zags and avoiding steep, direct ascents. I find them delightful and I regret that so little is being done to maintain them. I don't blame the estates for this — the need for the paths has decreased considerably — but surely those who gain such enjoyment from the hills, as we were on that hot July weekend, could do something to keep the paths in good working order?

The path up Sgurr Beag was as helpful as I had expected, and I bounded up the hill very happily. Peter was a little way behind, and confessed he was finding things a bit hard. It's odd how one performs in the hills. We all have up days and down days, seemingly without much in the way of logical reason. Over the course of a long trek this is particularly noticeable. It seems sometimes to be as much mental as physical, and once you've got it into your head that you're 'having a bad day' it's very difficult to shake that mood off.

Sgurr Mor was reached in time for a lunch stop. We talked about the rest of the day. I made the somewhat wild suggestion that we could reach the Tomdoun Hotel in Glen Garry, where we were to be picked up next day, that evening. This was quickly and correctly discounted as a possibility by Peter. Maybe the sun was getting to me! Another option was Kinbreack bothy in Glen Kingie. The problem there was that it would involve a two-mile diversion over ground that would all have to be recrossed in the morning, when our principal objective was Gairich, the last Munro in the chain we were traversing.

To keep to our straightforward eastern line was the simplest thing. This left the problem of the overnight stop. But really, in such weather conditions, was it a problem? We had no tent but we had good sleeping bags. Why not just bivouac out? 'Bivvying' is a great sport in itself and here we seemed to have an ideal opportunity to practice it. The decision was made. We would carry on over Sgurr an Fhuarain ('peak of the spring'), a summit of just under 3000 ft, and then drop down to bivouac between it and Gairich.

Between Sgurr Mor and Sgurr an Fhuarain we were treated to perhaps the most majestic sight the Highlands have to offer — an eagle soaring above us. The mastery of the air displayed by these great raptors is supreme. I shall never forget the shock I — and my dog — got once near the summit of another fine West Highland Munro, Beinn Sgritheall. We were picking our way down the mountain's northern ridge when an eagle got up almost

Glen Kingie from An Eag — where we saw the eagle (Roger Smith).

from under our feet — probably disturbed by the dog. Cloud and I stood transfixed as the massive bird wheeled above our heads and took off. Within a few seconds, so it seemed, it was across the glen and almost invisible. Our Sgurr Mor bird circled around for a few minutes, as if watching what we were doing, then apparently without effort leant on the air and crossed Glen Kingie, to be lost from our view. Humbled, we continued our slow progress.

On Sgurr na Fhuarain we both needed a good rest. No problem with this wonderful benison of sun blessing us — even if that same sun had caused our tiredness! Time passed. The effort needed to get up grew. We had to move, of course: bivouacing on Fhuarain's summit, without water, was not a good idea. We stumbled wearily down the steep eastern spur of the hill, looking for a suitable bivouac site. The ground on the bealach between Fhuarain and Gairich looked broken and boggy — not encouraging. A corrie a little to our left (north) seemed better in its lower reaches so we headed that way, taking care to skirt round several patches of dirty old snow left lingering from the very late spring. You can never tell what is under such snow patches and an injudicious step could land you in all sorts of trouble.

We found a very suitable site with a large flat boulder-top for cooking and enough level ground to lay our bags without undue risk of sliding down the hill. It was only 5.00 pm but we had had it, and after a very welcome brew we stretched out on our bags for a pre-prandial snooze.

There's nothing quite like bivvying for making you feel part of the hills, and I shall always remember that site under Gairich with affection. Not only was it a good bivvy in its own right, it gave us a grand evening watching the lengthening shadows changing the hill colours through a vivid spectrum from gold to russet red to tan to black, and it preceded one of the very finest mountain experiences it has been my privilege to enjoy. Bivouacing is very definitely a summer game in my book, and the long evenings of July are ideally suited for it. The only real problem (given dry weather, of course) is the pesky midge, the curse of Highland summer walking and camping, but we were relatively free of the little menaces that night.

We were asleep early, not only because we were tired but also to try to ensure a very early start on the Monday morning. When I woke I wasn't sure what sort of time it was. There was light of a sort but not the hard brilliance of the previous two mornings. Mist had rolled in during the night and visibility was confined to the immediate vicinity of our camp. I looked at my watch: 4.30 am. A good time to be stirring, so that we got our hill done early and could enjoy the walk out without time pressure. I woke Peter and we made a somewhat frugal breakfast, my gas canister having all but run out.

It took us a while to get packed and sorted and it was 5.45 am before we set off across the bealach to tackle Gairich. As we began the steep climb on to Gairich Beag, again helped by an excellent stalker's path, I was praying for one thing to happen. I forged ahead up the hill and at about 2,000 ft my prayers were fully answered. In one stride I went from a dim world of swirling mist into clean, bright sunshine. I knew then that what awaited us at the summit of Gairich would be worth all the effort of the previous three days added together.

It was. I almost ran up to the summit cairn in my excitement and joy at what spread before me: then like a child ran back to tell Peter to hurry to join me. Below us and to all the furthest horizons, cloud filled the glens. The mountain tops thrust through into the morning sunshine: a perfect temperature inversion had occurred, and the effect was magical. We gazed in wonder. Directly below us to the north, cloud swirled and eddied over Loch Quoich, revealing a shoreline for a second then hiding it again, to reveal another stretch a mile or two away. To the east a ray of sun had penetrated the mist and glinted on Loch Garry like some heavenly arrow.

To the south-east the jumbled hills of Lochaber shared the sunlight with us, and there again was Nevis, known to thousands of hillgoers simply as 'The Ben', its shape somehow very appealing from this distance. Across Loch Quoich, the broad shoulders of Gleouraich and Spidean Mealach filled the sky, the Affric giants diminished by distance behind them. I had one shot left in my camera. I use an automatic — how would it cope with this incredible sight? I lined Peter up by the cairn with Nevis next to him in the frame, pressed the shutter and prayed. Alas, the result was imperfect, not quite the *Great Outdoors* front

Above *Loch Quoich from Gairich, with the cloud beginning to lift. Sgurr a'Mhaoraich is the hill in the centre* (Roger Smith).

Right *Peter Evans on the summit of Gairich at 7.30 am, with the distinctive outline of Nevis visible just to the right of the cairn* (Roger Smith).

cover I had hoped for! Never mind, the scene is clearly enough imprinted on my mind's eye for photographic record to be unimportant.

After that it was all downhill — spiritually as well as physically. Apart from an enjoyable steep scramble for the first few hundred feet, the descent from Gairich was long and tedious — the more so when we again got embroiled in new forestry, in Glen Kingie, before meeting the track out. The navigational responsibility was mine and I seriously underestimated how long it would take us to reach Tomdoun. Nor did I realize how dull a trudge it would be through endless miles of conifer plantations. Forestry we must have, I agree, but surely it is possible to make it more attractive than this deadly stuff.

It was with a sense of some relief that we reached the Tomdoun Hotel, and it was an even greater relief to find that the bar was open. The first pint of shandy went down almost without touching the sides and a second quickly followed. Our 'chauffeur' Noel Williams — writer and member of the Lochaber mountain rescue team — duly arrived and ferried us back to Fort William. Our July trek was over. It had been a great success overall, with the early morning cloudscape below us from the summit of Gairich the highlight. We had celebrated a Highland midsummer in the best possible way.

July does not only mean long treks through the hills, however. It also means outings with the family into our local hills, the Ochils, taking a picnic up the very fine glen that cuts into the hills directly behind the small town where I live, to lie by the burn and laze away the afternoon watching dragonflies dancing over the water and hoping that one of the resident kestrels will thrill us with a display of hover and stoop that means death in the sun for some small creature and a meal for the falcon. It was only recently that I learned that, however gusty the wind, in the hover a kestrel's head stays absolutely still, showing extraordinary control of the air by this lovely bird.

Or we will go to one of the Trossachs lochs, which are less than an hour's drive away. A few years ago in a long dry spell the water level had fallen to such an extent that a large area of sand was exposed. This temporary 'beach' was eagerly commandeered by people like ourselves out for the day. As well as giving the children an excellent safe playground it provided interesting walking along a stretch which would normally be well under water!

July permits very long single-day outings to

The hills of Glen Kingie west of Tomdoun with Greenfield Bridge crossing the loch in the foreground (Hamish Brown).

Above *Looking north-west from Gairich as early morning cloud in the valleys begins to disperse* (Roger Smith).

Right *Looking back up to Gairich from the descent into Glen Kingie* (Roger Smith).

be taken, too. It is one of the favoured months for attempts on the Bob Graham Round, the circuit of 42 Lake District summits within 24 hours first achieved by Graham himself in 1932, not repeated until 1960, but now tried by dozens each year. I made the round myself in 1979, admittedly in June, and a memorable experience it was too. Being a continuous 24-hour circuit it perforce includes a night section, the long Helvellyn ridge being favoured for the ease of going underfoot. Night walking is another special summer occupation which can have a charm all its own, especially if you happen to be favoured with a good moon to help light your way.

There is a very peculiar feel to the hills at night. Your senses seem to become sharpened — perhaps returning to something like the state they were in many thousands of years ago before we became dulled by urban living — and impressions from your immediate surroundings take on a vivid importance they do not have by day. You are acutely aware of each footfall and the relative lack of background noise throws sounds up sharply as they occur.

I've done the stretch from Threlkeld to Dunmail Raise at night in July, assisting someone else on a Bob Graham attempt. You would expect to feel very tired on such a walk — after all, you are asking your body for a considerable effort at a time when it would normally be resting — but oddly that does not seem to happen. The heightening of the senses I mentioned earlier seems to ward off tiredness as well, at least until your walk is over. The whole experience takes on a dreamlike quality so that afterwards you wonder if it actually happened. It is impossible, I found, to estimate either time or distance and you seem to drift over the ground, feeling considerable surprise at arriving at some defined point such as a summit cairn.

July then is a month to look forward to — and to look back on, both anticipation and retrospection giving pleasure in equal proportions. I have for some years hankered after doing a very long traverse of the Cairngorms in summer, catching a train which gets to Kingussie at 3.00 am and walking via Glen Feshie and over the mighty tops of Cairn Toul and Braeriach and eventually back to Aviemore for an evening train home. Perhaps this will be the year I finally do it. Or perhaps not: there's a pleasure in the thought and the planning themselves.

We are all dreamers, we who wander the hills. It should be so. It enables me, sitting here writing this on a most dreadful day at the year's turn, with an easterly gale outside, lashing freezing rain horizontally across the hills, to turn my mind forward all the lengthening months to the other turn of the year, that time of greening when the wind's wild roar is replaced by birdsong and insect murmurs and when the freezing rain is gone and instead the sweet warmth of the high midsummer sun blesses us, the hill wanderers.

It should be so, for is it not the power of our dreaming that draws the year on through the dead months of winter to the new spring's first quickening, through the time of snowmelt when the burns are bloated and can kill to the time when they run quiet and low as if afraid to disturb the summer silence? It must be so, for us to survive days like this one, when it has hardly got light at all, when the wind makes sane men mad, and when the hills defy anyone to conquer them. On such days we must hold within us as an inextinguishable spark the knowledge of our dreams that in time, in good time, it will again be blessed July, the month of endless daylight.

Roger Smith was editor of *The Great Outdoors* **from the time the magazine was launched in 1978 until September 1987 when he took on the editorship of the new magazine,** *Environment Now.* **A four-season hill walker and backpacker whose other recreations include running and orienteering, he has lived in Scotland for ten years and in that time has become closely involved in the voluntary conservation movement. Born in London in 1938, Roger is married with two daughters. He has had ten books published on a variety of outdoor topics.**

An August journey down Memory Lane

KEVIN WALKER

In August 1969, four school friends and I spent a fortnight in the Brecon Beacons National Park on what was officially a 'Geological Expedition'. It was the first time I had been on an unsupervised, extended camping trip in a mountainous area and, to be perfectly honest, our enthusiasm for the mountains got the better of us, and the trip ended up as a veritable orgy of climbing and caving.

Towards the end of the 'geological expedition' we camped on the upper slopes of Mynydd Llangatwg, overlooking the picturesque town of Crickhowell. To cut a long story short, I fell in love with the place. Even in the innocence of youth I recognized that here was an area in which I could happily settle down. Little did I think that chance would lead me eventually to put down my roots less than five miles from where we pitched our tents. There's something about Mynydd Llangatwg! It's a huge mass of limestone almost 2,000 ft high which broods above the north-eastern corner of the South Wales Valleys. Capped with gritstone and peat, honeycombed with some of the longest cave systems in Britain, and with its edges nibbled away by past quarrying, it forms a barrier between the industrial and the agricultural to such an extent that it can almost be regarded as a cultural divide.

It is a place of opposites: of flat, boggy moorland and precipitous limestone cliffs; of untrammelled mountain wildness and the works of man. One hundred and fifty years ago the area echoed with the ring of hammer on stone, and a vast network of tramroads and inclines was constructed through the wilderness in order to connect both the ironworks of the Clydach Gorge and the Brecon and Abergavenny Canal with the quarries. A century before that, rugged packhorses bred from wild Welsh Ponies plodded up and down the slopes carrying lime from the quarries to the acid fields of the Usk Valley below. Five hundred years before the packhorses, local people — ancestors of one of the five 'Great Tribes' of Wales — chipped away at the surface rocks and outcrops in small 'public' quarries in order to build their farms and houses.

Nowadays the quarries lie deserted, their spoil heaps appearing as strange, knife-edged, grassy ridges, their faces either the playground of climbers or supporting a wide and varied flora, including some rare relics of the type of plant which grew in abundance at the southern

edge of the last glaciation. The tramroads lie neglected and overgrown, forgotten masterpieces of engineering offering easy walking into the heart of the area, but seldom visited by anything other than mountain ponies and the ubiquitous sheep.

Without a doubt, August is my favourite month on this mountain. Although much of it may have to do with nostalgia — a remembrance of the balmy expedition in the halcyon days of youth (read that as you will!) — I gain a certain satisfaction from wandering and exploring all day without the pell-mell jostling and sweaty crowds which usually accompany a walk in a classic area at the height of the holiday season. For a classic area it undoubtably is, with something for everyone. Add to that the fact that after ten years of regular use each step of the way brings a smile to my lips as memories of past visits spring to mind, and it is perhaps understandable that I count this as one of my favourite areas.

I remember one particular trip as if it were yesterday. Not only was it one of my rare 'days off' — August is usually the busiest time of year for me — but for once on a day off the weather was superb: hot without being sticky, with a gentle, fragrant breeze which carried with it the delightful summer smell of grass

Along the better preserved sections of tramroad one can see foundation stones, embankments and cuttings (Kevin Walker).

and heather. Having decided to spend all day on the mountain, crossing the cultural divide from south to north and generally wandering wherever my fancy took me, I cadged a lift with a fellow instructor who was taking a group caving in the Clydach Gorge.

Those of you who know the area may well think that this was a strange place from which to begin a peaceful and relaxed day's walking, but for me, setting out on what was to become a trip down memory lane, the dirty layby alongside the busy Heads of the Valleys Road was admirably suitable. In many ways it set the scene for what was to follow, for without the past industry which was centred in and around the Clydach Gorge, the mountain would not be the place it is today, nor would it have quite so much atmosphere.

The view from the layby was one I had seen countless times before — above the beechwood lay a chaotic conglomeration of abandoned quarries, linked together by stupendous tramroads and inclines which all seemed to defy gravity as they wound their unlikely way across precipitous slopes. Ironstone, coal, limestone and wood were once all easily accessible within this small area, and the ready availability of these raw materials

turned the gorge and its surroundings into the birthplace of the Welsh iron industry. During the last decade of the eighteenth century, a number of important ironworks were opened. As their appetite for materials increased, an extensive network of tramroads spread across the surrounding mountains like sinuous fingers grabbing for food.

I said goodbye to the group and sweated my way up the hill towards Brynmawr — the highest town in Wales. I have to admit that this was not the most pleasant experience of the day, for before I had gone half way, my head was reeling from the combined assault of exhaust fumes and the noise of heavy lorries. However, I caught occasional glimpses of picturesque waterfalls to either side as I walked, and these, combined with the knowledge that clean air and open moorland lay ahead, put a spring in my step which made passing motorists stare with amazement — or was it envy?

At the head of the gorge, the main road

The Llangattock escarpment, looking east. The lower tramroad is obvious below the base of the cliffs (Kevin Walker).

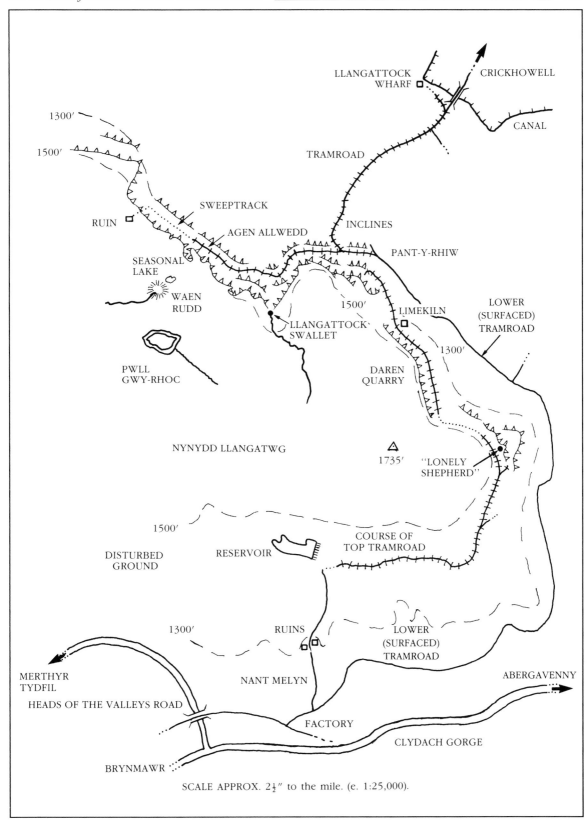

1300'

1500'

LLANGATTOCK
WHARF

CRICKHOWELL

CANAL

TRAMROAD

SWEEPTRACK

RUIN

AGEN ALLWEDD

INCLINES

PANT-Y-RHIW

SEASONAL
LAKE

WAEN
RUDD

1500'

LIMEKILN

LOWER
(SURFACED)
TRAMROAD

LLANGATTOCK
SWALLET

1300'

PWLL
GWY-RHOC

DAREN
QUARRY

NYNYDD LLANGATWG

1735'

"LONELY
SHEPHERD"

1500'

COURSE OF
TOP TRAMROAD

DISTURBED
GROUND

RESERVOIR

1300'

RUINS

LOWER
(SURFACED)
TRAMROAD

MERTHYR
TYDFIL

NANT MELYN

ABERGAVENNY

HEADS OF THE VALLEYS ROAD

FACTORY

CLYDACH GORGE

BRYNMAWR

SCALE APPROX. 2½″ to the mile. (e. 1:25,000).

ploughs its way through the landscaped spoil of years of cut and fill mining, eventually reaching its highest point at 1,350 ft. To my eyes, some of the landscaping looks worse than the original remains! My route lay above this, past a smelly computer disc factory, and along the now surfaced tramroad which contours around the eastern slopes of the mountain. Although popular with Sunday drivers, this is not a road for the unwary. Frost damaged each winter, it runs along the top of the steep, northern slopes of the gorge and at one point the driver can look down on the minute main road some 500, almost vertical, feet below!

Luckily the breeze was in my face, and a short way past the factory I could smell the moorland ahead. I left the lane at an ugly, quarried valley, and sauntered up the rough track towards the scanty ruins of Nant-melyn. I don't know why, but whenever I walk the middle section of this track, I always feel as if I am unwelcome, and spend most of my time looking over my shoulder. Much of it may have to do with my initial experience of the place: I met a bull which failed to appreciate my presence! The track is a public right of way (although you have to look at a map to realize it), and the landowner often grazes his cows here.

Theoretically, a bull in a field of cows is supposed to take more notice of the cows than he is of passing pedestrians, but nobody had told this bull how to behave. I don't know what breed he was — I didn't take much notice. All I can tell you is that he was big — very big and very fierce — and he seemed to be taking an inordinate amount of interest in me! I remember wondering whether I could outrun him in big boots: I also remember coming to the conclusion that I couldn't! Trying to walk nonchalantly along a rough track with one eye on a stamping bull and the other searching desperately for some form of defence is no easy task. In the end, I tried to cross the stream that runs parallel to the track. In doing so, I slipped on a rock and ended up sitting down in nine inches of water. This seemed to satisfy the brute who took no further interest in me!

Not far past the ruins, the track passes under some power lines and leaves the spoil behind. I climbed over a gate (it was locked and there was no stile) and there, spread out before my eyes, was the open moorland for which I had

been yearning. To my left, a broad expanse of bilberry and heather marched gently upwards towards the top of a spur, the surface criss-crossed with countless sheep tracks. To my right the ground fell away steeply towards the gorge, and my gaze swept almost automatically across the mountains on the far side, each one separating one of the industrial valleys from its neighbour. The valleys themselves may be industrialized, but the intervening ridges are wild and unkempt. Although they offer superb walking, they are seldom visited by anyone other than enthusiastic locals.

After a therapeutic gaze and a refreshing slurp from my flask, I scanned the land in front of me, looking for my next objective — the course of the first tramroad to be built across the mountain. It is easy to see. A broad embankment runs across marshy ground, one end destroyed during the construction of a nearby reservoir, the other end swept away by decades of winter storms. I once brought a group of environmental studies students past this point, and one bright spark insisted that the embankment was a glacial feature. He had a difficult time explaining the presence of dry stone walling along part of the route! No-one knows quite when this tramroad was built. It is known to have been in existence in 1818, and is thought to have had a gauge of 2ft 4in. Apart from that, little is known, and most of the history is pure conjecture for the documentation is very sparse.

When walking in the mountains, not just in this area, but all over Britain, I am continually astounded by the past works of industrial man. In every mountain area that I have visited, I have come across remains of past industry which defy the imagination and make me feel very humble. The sheer physical effort which must have been exerted for countless hours, day after day, week in, week out, in sunshine, rain and snow, make our modern way of life seem unbelievably easy and comfortable in comparison. And the effort and pride which went into their work still shows, for there is an atmosphere about all these mountain remains which I find fascinating to the extreme.

And yet there is a paradox here. If the tramroad were a modern railway, its magnetism would disappear and I would think it ugly and out of place. If I heard that the quarries were to be reopened to supply limestone for the Severn Barrage, I would try to block the move with every ounce of energy

Above *The Llangattock escarpment with one of the old tramways clearly visible as a linear scar about halfway up and parallel to the ridge* (Kevin Walker).

Left *In a few places the tramroad has subsided into the bog. Passing such obstructions involves either wet feet or a lengthy detour.*

I possess. Is it simply a function of age; the fact that the older works of man have been partially reclaimed by Mother Nature so that the rough edges have been rounded off, enabling us to see the achievement without the destruction? Or are there other factors at work?

I squelched across the moist ground to reach the embankment, then wandered on around the hillside, high and dry above the marsh. Scrabble down the far end, dance across the stream, then on and on, the views in front and to the right getting more impressive with every step, the mountain to the left becoming wilder yet more friendly.

The tramroad itself is better preserved the further one goes. After one more hiatus where it has subsided into a bog, it appears at worst as a level, green, short-grassed, path travelling across an otherwise rough and rocky grey-brown hillside. Along the better sections, the stones on which the spreaders or sleepers once

Right *The tramroad is littered with old foundation stones bearing the marks of the spreaders or sleepers* (Kevin Walker).

Top right *The clifftop path strays close to the edge in some places. It is in this area that the narrow descent path finds its unlikely way down through the precipices* (Kevin Walker).

Bottom right *This rocky, half-hearted cutting is at the centre of the cultural divide. On this side are the industrial valleys; on the other, the pastoral splendour of the Usk Valley.*

lay are still clearly to be seen, looking like a causeway of buried monoliths, their upper surface bearing drill holes and spreader-shaped indentations caused by the vibrations of heavily laden trams. There are shallow cuttings and low embankments with proudly constructed dry-stone sides, and where the track crosses the boulder fields, it is as though someone has scraped away the surface, rolled it flat, then painted it bright green.

In an effort to stay on level ground as much as possible, the tramroad makes a sweeping left turn around the mountain, hugging the 1,400 ft contour. As I turned the corner, the already superb view to the right became a veritable panorama, and I gazed out across the plains of Herefordshire and the ancient lands of the Marcher Lords. Mynydd pen y Fal, usually known as the Sugar Loaf, stood like a proud island in a patchworked sea, and the Skirrid — the Holy Mountain — appeared as if nestling below its flanks. Down on the plains, along the roads and in Abergavenny, all was bustle and noise as people went about their daily grind.

But up on the mountain, apart from the occasional distant thrum of a heavy lorry, I was surrounded by peace and tranquility.

A short way after the sweeping turn, a track drops down, past a lonely cottage, to the surfaced tramroad which I had left just after the factory. Ignoring this, I carried on past a few small quarries to a second junction. The first time I travelled this route, on a misty day not long after having arrived in the area, I carried straight on along the most obvious path, my head cowled in a cagoule hood, lost in a reverie and oblivious to my immediate surroundings. Suddenly, at my feet, there was nothing! I was standing at the top of a quarry and the ground dropped away sheer for about 100 ft. I don't know whether there had once been a hoist at this point, or whether an increase in the demand for limestone had caused the old tramroad to be quarried away (a common occurrence in this area). Either way, it was not a pleasant experience, but it did teach me to tread carefully across unknown ground.

On this occasion I ignored the obvious, and took a narrow track to the left which led into a quarried trough. At the far end was a half-hearted cutting through a rocky spur beyond which I could see nothing. Knowing what was to come, I hurried on with a delightful anticipation, scrambling across the bouldery floor like a young boy who has sensed some magic in the distance. However many times I walk this route, the view which appears on leaving the cutting always strikes me with a force which is so powerful as to be almost tangible. I removed my pack, sat down on the short, soft turf, leant back against a warm, friendly block of limestone, and gazed.

It is an enigmatic view. I am no Wordsworth, but I think that even the great poet would have difficulty in describing this scene. In front, and in profile, across a shallow valley, the mountain drops away in a convex slope towards the flat, green patchwork of the Usk valley. As it drops, the browns and purples become tans and duns, then hundreds of shades of green, each one richer than the last. Solitary rowans and clumps of hawthorn dot the scene with darker colour, and a near-horizontal band of outcrops and ancient quarries streaks across the landscape in contrasting shades of grey, from off-white to near-black. This is the start of the Llangattock Escarpment. And the feel of the breeze on my face... and the smell of heather and rock... and the sound of sheep and rustling grass...

To the right, on the far side of the Usk, the Black Mountains tower over Crickhowell, climbing in giant steps to their superb, rounded ridges. Knowing that I would get a better view of 'the Blacks' from a nearby vantage point, and wishing to visit the spot anyway, I dragged my gaze away from the escarpment and wandered over 'chossy' ground to the top of Darren Disgwylfa. Here stands the 'Lonely Shepherd' — an unquarried pillar of limestone which, according to local legend, is really a local shepherd who was turned to stone for mistreating his wife. The first time I saw it at close quarters it was unmarked. Imagine my horror to discover, on this occasion, that some misguided moron had decided it was an ideal site for spray-paint slogans, most of which were four–letter words. I do not understand how people can visit such a site only to defile it with their obscenities. So much for beauty and the human race.

Feeling saddened and cynical, I gazed across

From the clifftop path along the escarpment edge it is possible to look straight down into the Usk valley (Kevin Walker).

at the Black Mountains, the bare, white limestone on the summit of Pen Cerrig Calch gleaming like freshly fallen snow. Stumbling across motorcycle tracks, I decided that enough was enough, and strode back to my previous viewpoint, intent on enjoying the rest of my journey.

From here to the base of the first, low outcrops of the Llangattock Escarpment the tramroad is impossible to follow, having been destroyed when a gas-pipeline was laid across the mountain. Here, again, is the paradox. The tramroads and quarries seem a part of the scene; the disturbed ground of the pipeline, a scar across the landscape. Perhaps the answer

Close up, the shepherd is defaced by the barely literate (Kevin Walker).

The Lonely Shepherd with the white limestone cap of Pen Cerrig-calch just visible at left centre. The tramroad followed during the first section of the walk ends abruptly at the quarry face in the left lower third of the picture (Kevin Walker).

lies with 'modern' technology: the works of man are acceptable when they are done through his own effort whereas the works of mechanical diggers and machines are not. If only it was as simple as that.

By the time I reached the first outcrop and regained the tramroad, my cynicism had all but disappeared. I was now on home ground, for the escarpment is the equivalent of my office! I wandered along the track, poking into every nook and cranny — something I do habitually when walking in this area. When the quarrymen removed their stone, they uncovered countless holes, many of which are large enough to take the human frame, and some of which lead into cave systems. Being an avid caver, I am always on the lookout for new holes!

If I enthuse about the landscape above, I must also make mention of the landscape below, for caves are just as much a part of the environment and our natural heritage as are the mountains. In recent years the Llangattock Escarpment has become a focal point for cavers from all over the world, for beneath the mountain lie some of the finest and longest cave systems in Britain. It is now possible, for example, to travel from the escarpment to the Clydach Gorge entirely underground, passing beautiful formations and, for part of the way, travelling through the largest cave passage yet discovered in these islands.

As I passed the large Daren Quarry, I met up with society again. A group of wet-suited cavers was just about to go underground, forsaking the warm, August sunshine for the damp mysteries of the underworld. I continued towards the end of the tramroad, past the crumbling remains of an old limekiln, eventually entering Chwar Pant-y-rhiw through a narrow cutting surrounded by surreal ridges of grassy spoil.

Being the largest and most solid quarry on this side of the mountain, Pant-y-rhiw is much frequented by rock climbers. As it was the height of the holiday season, the flat-floored bay was teeming with people, some who had come to climb, others who were content simply to watch. About a century ago, when the quarry was operational, the quarrymen used to climb down chains fixed near the top of the working face, then hang on with one hand whilst prising away the stone with iron bars — a difficult and dangerous way to earn a living. A few links of one of the chains still

The network of tramroads around the Llangattock Quarries was once extremely complex. In the distance is Chwar Pant-y-rbiw, a popular climbing area.

hang in a corner of the quarry, and I wondered if any of the visitors had seen the rusting remains and, if so, whether they realized the use to which they were once put.

After the inevitable banter with a few friends, some climbing for pleasure, others for a living, I scrambled up the side of the quarry and turned my back on the real world once again. Toiling up the rough slopes towards the summit of the mountain, I thought of the cavers beneath my feet, imagining their awed whispers and cries of wonder as they came across glistening formations and delicate crystals growing from the living rock of the walls and the mudbanks of the floor. Remembering a caving trip of my own a few weeks previously, when a Peregrine falcon had flown close by as we emerged from the cave at dusk, I scanned the skies expectantly. A

it is possible to predict the mood of the mountain, to imagine in one's mind's eye the colours that will be seen. But in August such prediction is pointless, for the mountain changes from day to day and one never knows what colour awaits around the next corner. For me, it is this uncertainty, combined with the warmth and friendliness of the month, which gives August its unique character.

Leaving the cairn and the nearby trig point, I stumbled along the strange formations of bedrock, my mind dazzled by the greens and olives, the browns, beiges and purples of the surrounding moor. Keeping to the broad ridge, I watched spellbound as amorphous shadows chased each other across the embroidered plateau.

At the end of the ridge, lying just below the surface of the moor and hidden from view until one is quite close, lies Pwll Gwy-rhoc, a surprisingly large expanse of peat-black water. I have never seen this pool when it is still: whatever the time of year, whatever the weather conditions, there always seems to be movement. It is an eerie place, having a black atmosphere of its own. I have only camped beside its shore a few times, but on each occasion I have woken in the early hours and felt a certain something, a strange coldness — a sensation which I experience to a lesser extent even in the broad light of day. A major battle was fought somewhere on this mountain in the Dark Ages: I often wonder whether the pool marks the site, and what would be found if it were to be dredged.

Beyond the pool a sea of breeze-rippled grass stretched away towards the near horizon, beyond which I could just make out the distant, flat-topped summits of the Brecon Beacons. I wandered on across the moor, a tingle running down my spine as I turned my back on the lake, my feet eventually leading me to the top of a deep, narrow valley containing a dry river bed and bright green bracken. At most times of year, a musical mountain stream hurries down this valley to an area of rocks and boulders known as Llangattock Swallet. Here it disappears underground. It is an awe-inspiring sight when the stream is in spate.

On the far side of the swallet, the valley drops away in a series of steps, its sides clothed in short turf and dotted with lichen-covered boulders of white limestone and red-grey grit. Not yet ready to descend, I

buzzard soared serenely above the far end of the cliffline, but I could see no sign of the Peregrine. A shy bird at the best of times, there were probably too many people in the quarry for him to fly this way today.

I took my time reaching the summit. After all, the day was my own and it was only just turned noon. On arrival, having clambered up the final, boulder-strewn slope, I sat down in the minimal shade of an old beacon-cairn to have a salt tablet, a couple of handfuls of trail mix and a few slurps of tepid juice. As I gazed out over the wild, undulating gritstone moor which forms the top of the mountain, hazy clouds began to form overhead and the breeze brought with it the sweet green smell of approaching summer showers.

Whenever I am alone in the mountains, I tend to reminisce and ponder things both seen and unseen. This day was no exception. I thought back over the previous decade, smiling at past trips and experiences, remembering different seasons, different colours, different moods. At most times of year

The lower tramroad wends its way into the heart of the impressive Llangattock escarpment (Kevin Walker).

scrambled up a short but steep spur to an area of gritstone boulders and large shakeholes — crater-like depressions formed where surface rocks have collapsed into the caves below. A quarter of an hour later, I reached the top of the Llangattock Escarpment and sat on a jutting prow of rock which is one of my favourite viewpoints. I was on the lip of nothingness at the edge of eternity.

Fourteen hundred feet below but less than two miles distant lay the Usk valley, its main road choked with caravans and cars. On the far side rose the southern bastions of the Black Mountains, their ridges flowing into the

northern skies towards the distant wilderness of mid-Wales. As impressive as this panorama was, it did not catch the attention nor inflame the senses anywhere near so much as the rich, verdant precipices of the scarp stretching away to either side.

To the west, horizontal bands of vertical, pale grey limestone dropped suddenly from the flat plateaulands above, each cliff separated from its neighbour by lines of scree or tree-filled gullies, each tier merging into the next in a series of ledges which were dark green with vegetation. To the east, the upland moorland dropped in an ever steepening convex slope,

October: *As the track snakes up the Khumbu valley the magnificent peak of Ama Dablam comes into the traveller's view* (Walt Unsworth).

October: *The fall carpets the Vermont woods with brightly coloured leaves* (Walt Unsworth).

October: *The autumn tints of trees along the lakes in Britain's Lake District can compete with those anywhere in the world. These trees line the banks of the Rothay near Ambleside* (Walt Unsworth).

October: *New England in the fall: the Camel's Hump in the Green Mountains of Vermont* (Walt Unsworth).

Left November: *The Quantock ridgeway is an ancient path of character and interest to the hiker, especially in early November as the leaves collect at one's feet* (Brian Atkin).

Left November: *On the Quantocks in late November a rainbow draws attention to one of the many coombs which run off this unusual southern English plateau* (Brian Atkin).

Below November: *A showery day with sunny spells brings out the winter colours of the Quantocks, here near Dowesborough* (Brian Atkin).

Right December: *Pen-y-Ghent becomes an icy fortress standing proud against the skyline and visible from many parts of the Western Dales* (Colin Speakman).

Right December: *An icy River Wharfe rushes past the icicles on its rocky banks near the Strid* (Colin Speakman).

Below December: *In winter sunlight this attractive bridge near Hawes stands timeless: functional but completely harmonizing with its location* (Colin Speakman).

its base marked by vertical rock, its mid-slopes castellated by jutting buttresses of near-white limestone. The mountain drops 600 ft in as many yards, and it is this sudden demarcation between wild upland and tamed lowland that I find so impressive.

I wandered westwards along the edge of the cliffline as if in a dream, but being conscious all the time that I should not let familiarity breed contempt. The narrow, sometimes rocky clifftop path strays within inches of the edge in parts, and this can be a dangerous place for the unwary or foolhardy. However, the views along this section of cliff are unparalleled and, to my mind, the walk along the top is the best of its kind in Britain.

Reaching the top of another steep-sided valley which cuts its way into the edge, I forsook my clifftop wandering for a short while to visit Waen Rudd, a stupendous shakehole some 200 ft wide and almost 100 ft deep. Like Llangattock Swallet, this is an even more impressive spot after heavy rain, for a stream pours from the plateau and falls to the base of the hole where it disappears. Today the stream was almost dry, only a slight trickle tinkling down the rocks, and the nearby seasonal lake was a dusty mattress of peat. How different from my last visit when, after a wet and stormy night in a nearby sheltered campsite, only just large enough for my tent, I emerged in time to see the dawn sun casting rainbows in the spray which was whipped from the falls by the wind.

After another munch and a quick slurp it was back to the cliff edge and westwards once again, past the tops of trees which grow from ledges on the cliff face below. From this elevated viewpoint it is possible to see not only the patchwork of the present field boundaries, but also darker lines across individual fields which show where old

The distant Sugar Loaf, as seen from the side of the massive shakehole of Waen Rudd. The black patch just right of centre is the peaty bed of a seasonal lake (Kevin Walker).

boundaries once were.

Eventually I descended into a shallow, semicircular basin shaped something like a broken saucer, the broken edge of which represents the lip of the escarpment. There are numerous small shakeholes in this area, two of which contain the entrances to small caves, others which are littered with plastic fertilizer bags which I can only assume have been blown here from the fields below! Right in the centre of the basin, close to a cairn, lie the enigmatic ruins of a small, stone shelter, most likely built decades ago by a local shepherd.

The rocky cairn marks the start of a narrow path which somehow finds its way through the cliffs to meet up with the end of yet another tramroad — an extension, in fact, of the surfaced tramroad I had left at Brynmawr earlier that same day. As I descended, I was thankful that the day had kept fine, for the surface of what is little more than a loose sheep track can become lethally muddy in wet weather, and the prospect of a fall is not a pleasant one. Indeed, I have known people travel a fair distance to the east or west in

search of a descent route, rather than tread this vertiginous path. One has to stop to admire the views; to walk and look at the same time would be sheer lunacy.

As I scrabbled down the final, quaggy section and on to the friendly, level tramroad which traverses the cliffs like a wide ledge, I heard the clang of a heavy iron gate being opened, and a party of tired, wet and muddy cavers emerged from Ogof Agen Allwedd (or Aggie, as it is affectionately known), screwing up their eyes at the brightness. One of the longest caves in Britain, with almost twenty miles of passage found so far, it has been designated a Site of Special Scientific Interest and has therefore been gated by the Nature Conservancy Council. The keys are freely available to bona-fide cavers, and the cave is justifiably popular.

Knowing both the cave and, on this occasion, the cavers, we wandered along the tramroad together, swopping stories of the day's events both overground and underground. Even though we all knew this section of tramroad like the backs of our hands, there were still comments about particular views or about the way the light was hitting a buttress. After a pleasant plod, we stopped at the top of an incline which drops steeply towards a forestry plantation, and investigated the sparse remains of the brake wheel pit and the brakeman's hut, connected by a small, square, stone–lined hole through which the brake rod once passed.

After half an hour of prodding, conjecture and hilarity, they wandered off along the tramroad towards their nearby club cottage, and I prepared myself for the descent of the incline — a quick way back to Crickhowell, but not too kind on the toes! When the incline was first built, it was used as a shoot, which will give you some idea of the angle. However, the hurtling stones did so much damage to the retaining walls that it was eventually converted into a proper incline!

Reaching the bottom, I tightened my boots, and set off down the second, longer incline which drops 300 ft in 1,800 ft, its surface loose and worn. Glad to reach the bottom, I climbed over the stile, and followed the tramroad through a delightful section of green and fragrant woodland. Squirrels and rabbits bounded away at my passing, but the sounds of a mountain summer were soon to be shattered by the horrendous noise of a valley campsite. I was back in civilization again, and my greeting was a cacophony of blaring radios and cassette players, each one trying to drown out the mindless noise of the other.

I hurried past the site and soon reached a relatively quiet country lane, still on the track

Far left *The lower tramroad cuts its way across the steep slopes of the Llangattock escarpment* (Kevin Walker).

Left *The gated entrance to Ogof Agen Allwedd, one of the longest caves in Britain* (Kevin Walker).

Llangattock Wharf and the lime kilns on the Brecon and Abergavenny Canal: the termination of the bottom section of the tramroad (Kevin Walker).

of the tramroad. The lingering smell of exhaust fumes was in the air, so I lifted my pack higher on my shoulders and plodded on with my own thoughts until I reached the narrow bridge over the Brecon and Abergavenny Canal. Here was the reason for the inclines, for the tramcarts which travelled them brought stone from the quarries to the limekilns at Llangattock Wharf.

Fifteen minutes later having, where possible followed narrow alleys and footpaths rather than the road, I walked through Crickhowell and into the Bear just as the towels were being removed from the pumps. 'Good day?' asked Steve, pulling my pint without needing to ask what I wanted.

I smiled. 'It's August, isn't it?'

Kevin Walker lives near Crickhowell in Powys, on the edge of the Brecon Beacons National Park. An honours graduate in Occupational Psychology, he has worked as a freelance mountain activities instructor for over ten years, and is a regular contributor to *The Great Outdoors*. His first book, *Mountain Navigation Techniques*, was published in 1986 and there are others in the pipeline!

September's slack between the tides

JIM CRUMLEY

September, when it is most true to itself, is the slack water in the ebb and flow of the seasons, lying like a brim-full tidal pool amid the rock and wrack of the wild year, betraying barely a trace either of the ebb of summer or the gathering forces of the flow of autumn. But that same September, when it is honest to itself, is a rarity in Highland Scotland. There are Septembers which taunt and tantalize with taste and aftertaste of any season you care to name, and there are those most fickle of September days which can stun and startle you with all four.

In the earliest September days, ospreys wheel and go, trailing south a wake of spring and summer echoes, leaving me to forage through the littered images of those earlier seasons like a squirrel among beech roots so that I might amass an osprey store to see me through from September to spring. I have come too close to ospreys, perhaps. I can pace the stone shore of my osprey loch in early September and find it a forlorn place full of the fits and false starts of human sentiment which have no place, I am told, in nature's relentlessly defined and redefined scheme of wild things. In September he goes. In April he returns. Be grateful that he has been. Be grateful that he returns. But September is an uneasy fretful month on the osprey-empty shore, at least until its last few days when nature contrives huge compensations, flung from the far north, of wild geese and wild swans. For the intervening weeks, I have

September is an uneasy, fretful month on the osprey-empty shore (Jim Crumley).

devised a cure for my illness of sentiments. I go north, tortuously, to meet their south-journeyings.

It will begin with a point on my old familiar mountain skyline. It is far from the highest point and far from the lowest, but close to the bonniest, and depending how you go, the wildest. If you sidle along Achrayside marking the first paling of larch, the first curling of bracken, the blood-letting of rowan, and thrust through the Commission's forest, you find yourself between Katrine's shore and the ragged north wall of Ben Venue.

Here is the kernel of the Trossachs, the showy shell cracked open and cast, a wild enough, romantic enough, rough enough tumble of hillside to appeal to both Walter Scott and ring ousels: both have an unerring eye for landscape. It is a better way down the mountain than up it, but given that the unkind combination of waymarking and the print of summer hordes have reduced Ben Venue's main thoroughfares to something more reminiscent of Scafell Pike or a festering Skye peat bog I know, the purgatory of this climb is softened by the knowledge that it is the route most in keeping with the spirit of the mountain.

It is warm for a north-facing hillside in September, warmer than anything which July or August divined, but there is new gold tipping the deer grass so that the burnish of summer on my back is taunted and tempered by the burnish of autumn beneath my feet. It is no less of a paradox of September to say that the day feels like neither season, and that for the fleeting moments in the mountain's life which are the hours of my climb, both mountain and climber are September blessed. But far over my right shoulder and Ben More's left, there is the first small swelling of a black bruise and the promise that before the day is done this seasonless month will parade all the treacheries in her fickle repertoire.

I have shed the deer path for a gully of

Ben Venue — the wind lays siege to mountain ramparts (Jim Crumley).

Highland jungle, a place so wrapped and raptured by bracken, rowan, heather, moss, lichen, alder and stunted runts of oak and golden silver birch that for twenty minutes of gully dawdling there was no shred of rock or scree in sight. But I was lured here by the old familiar soft cackle of the ring ousels, and there are few diversions I wouldn't contemplate for the privilege of watching these birds at close quarters. I settle into a small hollow of heather and blaeberry, overhung with berry-groaning rowans. The cock bird's alarm is a false one, for the mountain blackbird has the curiosity and courage of a weasel. His occasionally fatal fearlessness in the face of peregrine or buzzard is no less characteristic than a readiness to turn a blind eye on a rock-still human.

He returns in two minutes, berry laden, his approach heralded by the emergence from a screen of rowan of two unsuspected young birds. The fact that they are still being fed by the adults suggests that what passed for summer has induced a late second brood. Six weeks from now, if the neighbourhood peregrines spare them, they will contemplate their first winter in the Mediterranean. Miracles in the Highland world of birds are commonplace. They might pause in their berry foragings there to mob a young osprey with which they have more in common than they will know...

A small silver lochan lies like a locket on the bosom of this mountain, a place of bog cotton, reeds and wide northern horizons. A goosander loses its nerve behind a veil of reeds, hurdles the rock lip of the lochan and rises to circle higher and higher, flaring and dowsing deep and dark cream as he flies from sun into shade and into sun again and again. It is only when I drag the glasses across that far skyline bruise and see how it has swollen and advanced that I speed the climb to the summit.

By the cairn there is a flat eerie calm of the kind which concentrates the susceptible hill mind, permits penetration beyond the fabric of the mountain itself, and like the swirl of a warm cloak about your shoulders offers moments as long as aeons, absorbs you into the clan of hill spirits. I frankly believe in such things, believe they are accessible to those who honestly seek them in the times and places where human and landscape rhythms coincide, a handful of days in a life-ful. I now find them here. Secrets, understandings are told and offered. From these you deepen your appreciation of the value of wildness. They are the glittering prizes for the wilds-wanderer who chooses to go alone, because in their company and with the knowledge they bring, alone is the one thing you will never be.

Then some fickle God of the Wilds commands 'Enough' and effects the unlikely intrusion on a Highland summit of a country dance band stepping deftly through the intricacies of a reel which I can't put a name to for the moment. If there had been a swirling of mists around the cairn, or if the hill had been drenched in one of those clammy 'smirry' days which can suspend all notions of time and place, those same susceptibilities of stillness might have conjured imagery in the gloom of ragged fugitive musicians, two dimensional children of the mist reliving their last agonies in the flight from Sheriffmuir. But if you glare down at the loch on such a sunlit day as this, or if you have sat here in all weathers and seasons as I have, you know the intruder to be the PA system on the *Sir Walter Scott* as it steams the last of the season's tourists across the poet's 'lake', by kind permission of the water board. Romance in the Trossachs is not what it was.

September's next trick is a little dirtier. The Crianlarich hills are suddenly no longer a part of the northern skyline, and that black sky has hurried south and lowered its base to about 1,000 ft, the more evil because the sun still blithely lights its progress. The quick way down assumes a critical importance, but 100 ft below the summit, the thing rushes down in a frantic blizzard.

No snow at this time of the year lasts for long, so I deny the instincts of retreat and savour the majestic elemental montrousness of what is happening from the lee of a small crag. In five minutes the summit is white. In ten, it has vanished under a torment of winds and snow whipped and whirlpooled up into spindrift the instant it lands, the whole frantic symphony underpinned by the unbroken percussive roar of the winds laying siege to mountain ramparts. But true to form, September giggles at the wrath of the storm by gnawing the battered rag-and-tatter clouds with fleeting glimpses of baby blue skies to the south and west...

It took 25 minutes for the storm to cross the mountain. Ben More and Stobinian re-emerged looking like January, but by dusk there would be nothing to show for September's sorcery. I

The Crianlarich hills from high on Ben Venue with the Sir Walter Scott *plying its way across Loch Katrine below* (Jim Crumley).

turned down to confront the mortal world again. In the gully ring ousels gorged on, draining the rowan tree's blush. On the *Sir Walter Scott*, the band plays on, and on, and on.

All my north-westerings are likely to be foot-faltering, side-tracking, back-watering affairs in which I can kill an hour or a day in the spontaneous rekindling of old landscape preferences and the cultivation of new ones. An old one is a small loch in Glen Dochart which in its due season harbours and holds a hundred Whooper swans, and although that season is still two, perhaps three weeks off, there is always the possibility even in mid-September of an advance guard riding a tail wind. Frail as the hope may be, the fact that it germinates on one of those exclusively September-lit mornings when the air has an almost crystalline clarity is excuse enough to haul in by Ben More, slip beneath the road to an instant wilderness. The road west rumbles blindly on behind.

Here, lingering, I have wrecked whole mountain expeditions and emerged hours later

with no more than two miles beneath my boots, my wilderness integrity intact, my conscience clear. There are whole mountains — Munros even! — I would trade for lochs like this and their wild hinterlands, where almost anything can turn up and often does. And unlike the osprey loch, I can take to these shores even in the lack-lustre Whooperless days.

Today is one of these. There are white-prowed autumn heralds afloat but goldeneye and tufted duck cluster beneath that far buttress-and-birch shore, pied patchworks of birds which adjust querulously to the wing-flashing crash landing of five wigeon. A large dark buzzard drops from easy spirals on higher crags into their flightpath, but pulls out well short of the water. Perhaps this one was impressed by some vagrant sea eagle's passing flair and is having difficulty coming to terms with the less amphibious skills of his own tribe. Perhaps.

That wildest far shore of the loch is a thigh-deep river away, which keeps passing humanity at bay. There may be a few others who are willing to work for the prize of this sanctuary but I never see any beyond the river. The more relentless the march of the manufactured countryside of parks and footpaths and high-rise forest invades Scotland, the more diligent I become in search of what remains of my own definition of wildness, the more I cherish that which I discover. The imported bureaucratic philosophy which dilutes wildness has no place in the Scottish tradition. Its most unforgiveable crime is to diminish — even deny — the joy of discovery by contriving pre-packed, processed order out of nature's majestic disorder. The more we distance ourselves from the land, the more we distance ourselves from what our forebears would recognize as our species.

Such thoughts slip easily into place in an eyrie of my own, high on the loch's north shore. I have been sitting here a long hour now watching a group of forty hinds and calves, eavesdropping on their red deer smalltalk, the calm before the storm of the rut which is October. In my sitting, watching and listening I have achieved nothing other than the establishment of a personal perspective on these deer in their own domain. For me it is an achievement of some value — that and the satisfaction of arriving and leaving undetected.

The river *is* Glen Orchy. There are no nursery miles for the Orchy, no fledgling flocking of hill burns marching on a fraternal crusade for the sea. It flows full bodied and mature of urge and surge from womb to wake, from Loch Tulla to Loch Awe; swerves mightily into its glen and ploughs a furrow of dark-deceptions through its generous girth.

Ben Inverveigh holds sway over the glen's north-east portal, held thrall over the young Duncan Ban MacIntyre's gaze, a fit land for poets. Now the thrall holds good over my own

---

Glen Orchy from Ben Inverveigh: 'Light floods in at the far end of the glen, spreads its benevolent stain upriver...' (Jim Crumley).

gaze. September is in its sorcerer's mood. The sun has finally beaten a path through cloud-crammed skies, torched the crown of Beinn Udlaidh across the glen, lit the river for golden miles but thrust the bulk of the hills into unfathomable silhouette. The sky retreats and light floods in at the far end of the glen, spreads its benevolent stain upriver, draining the water of its fires mile by slow mile. By the time it has reached my hill, Glen Orchy has changed colour and character. Behind, the hills of the Blackmount have caught their own Midas mood, an untypical burnishing of dark gold. Orchy's hills stand back from their river, a brooding respect infringed only by the bank-hugging instincts of alder and hazel. These pay the price of their daring from time to time where the bank succumbs to the gnawing water, or a spate snaps a trunk or drags a shallow root into a turmoiled oblivion. It's a bank-trembling, awe-inspiring river at close quarters, fearsome in spate, but from my river-watcher's eyrie on Ben Inverveigh it looks a benign enough water, glittering through the late afternoon.

I have many reasons to be grateful to this corner of Argyll. For years now these have been my mountain-shoulders-to-lean-on, my quiet, thought-gathering acres. More than any other corner of the Highlands, this is my back-

Above *Ben Venue from Loch Achray: the dramatic interplay of sky, mountain, loch and time* (Jim Crumley).

Right *Ben Tee magnificently reflected in Loch Garry* (Hamish Brown).

of-the-hand glen, a landscape with which I have won a cherished familiarity so that it wraps me round and embraces my thoughts. Of all its seasons and summits, though, I love it best in the long lull of seasonless September, and on this summit, which, if you walk in from Inveroran, saves the whole sudden spread tapestry of Glen Orchy for the last few steps to the cairn. There are few glens I am happier to see beneath my feet.

My attention wanders to the skies — I have greeted the south-wintering Whoopers on this hill before now, but this day yields no more than a prospecting buzzard over the highest trees. It is a fact of these half-hearted goose-and-whooper hunts that they have become an expeditionary excuse with no expectation, but once by that lochan at the head of Coire Orain, the corrie of songs, they called my bluff and sent me three high-bugling swans halfway through September. No corrie ever sang sweeter.

Glencoe is a shroud where the deer mope and the deer grass catches your eye suddenly under your feet. It has bronzed, and September has lurched out of its daydream. The Ben is lost, not only head in the clouds, but also its neck, shoulders, torso, skirts and foothills. Glengarry hisses softly where the road and the soup steam in the rain and weird wisps of cloud move among still trees on airless winds. By Loch Garry a tiny rowan grows from a rock, and as it thrives by different rules from the rest of its tribe, wears leaves of red and no berries. Kintail bares only three-and-a-half Sisters but there is a gleam in the sky again, so I lift over Ratagan and ginger down the hairpins to my shore of shores.

'For I am convinced,' wrote Gavin Maxwell here, 'that man has suffered in his separation from the soil and from the other living creatures of the world; the evolution of his intellect has outrun his needs as an animal, and as yet he must still, for security, look long at some portion of the earth as it was before he tampered with it.' This is a place which is almost too hard for me to take for its barely believable beauty, its overburdening sadness, and the indelible imprint of Maxwell's magnificently misguided life. His otter stories travelled the world — they still travel it almost twenty years after his death — but it is in his writing about landscape that he touched heights, probed depths and fashioned philosophies with unrivalled literary lucidness.

Always when I climb Beinn Sgritheall I climb by the Allt Mor Santaig — the burn of the waterfall, the soul of Camusfearna he called it, that glittering arc which prompted Kathleen Raine's now immortalized poem to begin:

'He has married me with a ring, a ring of bright water...'

A view across Loch Garry, near Tomdoun (Hamish Brown).

Dawn over Loch Hourn from Beinn Sgritheall (Jim Crumley).

The burn flirts with the overworld and the underworld to the last summit rocks of the mountain, and it is difficult not to imbue its first infant stumblings into daylight with a kind of creative reverence, the fount of a rare perception of our wild places. From here the waters spill away to Sandaig, to the lighthouse islands, to mingle their sweetness with Loch Hourn's salt, to voyage in the Sound of Sleat, to wash ashore at a far lighthouse. Maxwell followed its course to Isle Ornsay in the last chapter of his life's adventures. My own September north-westerings stumble sooner or later with a willing and inevitable tread from this shore to that. These hills are Maxwell's 'plum-red distances'. My Skye.

Skye weeps. The third day dawns like the first two, as reluctant as a hedgehog in January, as sluggish as a duck in mud. Rain flows in vertical tides, warm and windless, soft and ruthless, from first light to last. The high moor above Bracadale oozes like a sponge through every peat-black pore. The Snizort, never the most expressive of rivers, swells and grins at its trembling banks with barely suppressed ill-tempered might.

I make what I can of such an island day by following the angler's path deep into the moor, but find the river's mood catching, so that when I break my own subdued silence it is to curse the underfoot treacheries of the sodden land. A straight line short-cut to counter one of the river's long loops is a bad idea. An overtrousered leg sinks in peat up to its overtrousered thigh. By the time I regain *terra firmish* I wear the colour and the equilibrium of temperament of a rutting stag without hinds. Onward...if only for a way of passing the day. Tomorrow may be a gem, and I will have this day's weary drapery to set it against, the more to admire its finery.

Five mallard leap from my path, more, I am sure, in astonishment at my presence in such a place on such a day than from any sense of alarm. I follow their flight, the only moving things in that bowl of grey gloom that isn't water in one of its torturing guises. As they wheel and fly back above me, I fumble for the glasses, catch up with the birds fifty yards downstream, lose them to the circling drenching curtains of rain and mist 100 yards away, and moan morosely that freeing the glasses was not worth what now seems utterly unreasonable effort.

But they are out now, and I swing them through the points of the compass in a long, slow sweep of the horizon-free world. Somewhere between north and south-south-

The River Snizort swears its innocence and tranquil intentions beneath a perfect September sky (Jim Crumley).

east I drag past a discernibly mobile fragment of hillside, reverse the sweep of the glasses, and find a moor-quartering golden eagle. Friend of the wilderness Mike Tomkies' advice to me about eagle watching — 'learn to scan the middle distance' — has long since been burned into the psychology of my mind's eye as an instinctive response to high wild places. Here, it was never so easy — there is only middle distance. I have often had cause to value Mike's friendship. Now as I focus on that spreadeagling of dark wings, the day's burdens slip from my shoulders in avalanches.

I watch her work the ground for ten minutes, during which time she is never more than six feet above the moor — often less — and never touches it. The leisurely control of the flight, 'the achieve[ment] of, the mastery of

the thing', the restraint of power, the flawless fluency, the calculated purpose, are everything the river is not. I follow her in the glasses, eyes and arms aching now, until she suddenly cut-and-thrusts up at the rains, climbs the storm and is gone.

I console my long, leaden walk out with her recalled flight and recall other eagles on far hillsides, and the eagle trekking, writing and talking of Mike Tomkies. These are fit companions to light a spark in the drab and suddenly cloister-cold afternoon, to see me through until dusk when my last rainward glance catches a pale yellow shredding of the northern sky over Rona. By midnight the sky is a heaven again, star-stippled.

Skye dances. The fourth day dawns with the promise of that true September, a vivid sequin

A place of contemplation, peace and quiet, the gentle banks of the River Snizort can actually be boggy and treacherous (Jim Crumley).

of a day which flashes on all Skye's waters with a unique island flair. Walter Poucher, crown prince of mountain photographers, used to eulogize about the light in Skye. 'Nature's masterpiece of the Hebrides', he once called it, and on those truest of September mornings, it is a phenomenon of unfathomable clarity. Now on the same riverbank of yesterday's rain-prison, sprawls a matchless skyline: the Cuillin silhouettes to the south, leaping as abrupt above the moor as pyramids from sand. From the high moor above Bracadale the Outer Isles and their hills laze in sparkling seas. Dark tiny silhouettes, impossible distances west prick horizons and send me stumbling through mental geographical somersaults — St Kilda? Impossible. Yet if not that, what...?

With the question unresolved I drop back towards a reedy fold in the river now turned as demurely submissive as yesterday's was overbearing. If my day's walking had been a haphazard affair thus far, these last few steps down off the moor are surely predetermined, some subconscious beckoning to the unseen foraging of the new season's first vanguard Whooper swans. One suddenly alert head comes above the crest of the bank; then two birds wheel in midstream, thresh the air and the water with the controlled orderly panic of retreat, run six small strides on the surface of the river, and fly, white gods of my wilderness, following the watercourse deep into heart of the moor.

My good September omen.

Skye sleeps in. The fifth day — the last day — dawns still as a spider's web in a drizzle. A

The matchless skyline... Cuillin silhouettes with the River Snizort picked out as a silver thread below (Jim Crumley).

'smirry' hint of rain passes on, leaves the bay a glittering grey. I walk above one of those unsung bays of Sleat when the blunt-headed, bubble-tailed wake of a hunting otter cuts the surface. A head rises, gazes, dives, and the arc of mustelloid body and tail follows in perfect splashless ritual.

From here it is easy: the glasses pick up the bubbles, and sooner or later he surfaces, five or six feet ahead of them, flips on to his back and with 'hands' and jaws, gorges himself on flatfish, eels, crabs caught seemingly at will. I curse the telephoto lens for succumbing to a Perthshire bog three weeks previously. The 40 mm lens I'm stuck with is useless at this range. So I change the rules.

He swims directly for the rocks below me now, his wake broadened and blunted by the bulk of crab in his jaws. He comes ashore on a shelving rock, where just above the highest lap of the highest imperceptible wave, be begins to grind the crab to little more than shell sand. I slither down the grass covered cliff, cross a strip of shingle to the big rocks, and crawl, flop, crab, flounder to within twenty feet of him. Now the camera is a realistic proposition. The sound of his teeth on the shell is clear on the still air. Focus, press the shutter; wind on, press; wind on, press ... at the third shutter click he spins round on his rock, hisses a breathy 'haaaah!' which I answer with what otter disguise I can muster. This banal mono-syllabic exchange goes on for twenty minutes, during which time he catches another crab. This one is landed on a different rock. I stalk him again, and the ritual is re-enacted. Haaah! or Hah! or Haaaaaaahhhh! he warns the camera, till he tires of its stubborn clicks, takes to the bay at speed, and is lost to the headland.

On my last hour on the island, I cross the headland again. There is no otter, but high overhead, I hear the first strains of goose-

Sgurr Mor and the hills on the edge of Knoydart—seen across Loch Quoich (Hamish Brown).

speech. A skein of twenty, flying high, driving south-west, cross the shore, the Sound, and fly deep into the heart of Knoydart.

There are times in places like that last quiet hour when the power of landscape can move me to an almost religious fervour. It has become the religion of my life, and I find neither surprise nor superstition in those tribes of ancients who placed their Gods in mountains. I am never easy when I leave Skye, but I am consoled these last lingering September days by the knowledge that the Whooper and the goose are ahead of me, that when I confront the shore of my osprey loch again, they will welcome me as I welcomed them here. In our own ways, we keep the wild faith. September wanes. The tide turns and flows again.

Jim Crumley was born in Dundee in 1947. He is a journalist by profession, and is currently chief feature writer for the Edinburgh *Evening News*: he was Scottish Feature Writer of the Year in 1985. He is also Scottish area reporter for *The Great Outdoors* and is the current chairman of the Scottish Wild Land Group, which he helped to found in 1982.

October and the opening of new wine

WALT UNSWORTH

'Between thirty and forty one is
    distracted by the Five Lusts;
Between seventy and eighty one is prey
    to a hundred diseases.
But from fifty to sixty one is free from all
    ills;
Calm and still — the heart enjoys rest.
I have put behind me Love and Greed, I
    have done with Profit and Fame;
I am still short of illness and decay, and
    far from decrepit age.
Strength of limb I still possess to seek the
    rivers and hills;
Still my heart has spirit enough to listen
    to flutes and strings.
At leisure I open new wine and taste
    several cups;
Drunken I recall old poems and chant a
    stray verse.'

from On Being Sixty by Po Chu-i

In the springtime of life a young man's fancy turns to rock-climbing, or at least mine did. Along with some like-minded companions I would catch the bus or train to some local outcrop such as Helsby and there let the adrenalin flow freely as my rock boots smeared on exiguous holds. Later on came the time of starlight and storm; the high summer of alpine endeavour. I still shiver at the memory of a bivouac on the Frontier Ridge of Mont Blanc, waiting for the first green light of the pre-dawn, and I remember my nervous probing of a tenuous snow-bridge on the Mittelberg Glacier, hoping it wouldn't collapse whilst I was on it. Those were the days of the Matterhorn and the Zinal Rothorn, the Chardonnet and fifty or sixty more glorious summits. There is still the odd climb, the occasional summit, but life moves on like the year itself until even the September song is just a memory.

Fortunately, as old Po Chu-i points out in his poem, the October of life is a golden period, not unlike the month itself. Ambition of the earlier sort is stilled. You know now that you will never climb the Eigerwand or Everest and the nice thing is that it doesn't seem to matter any more. No doubt there is still the odd flicker of special effort; the occasional feeling of delicious guilt when you step on something too hard or too high and perhaps a last despairing ambition to climb all the Munros: the ultimate graveyard of mountaineering hopes. But mostly it is a time for trying new wine, or old wine in new bottles.

Mountaineers who are worth their salt have done a lot of walking throughout their careers, but it is only now that it begins to take on proper meaning. It lies at the heart of the matter. I am not speaking of those huge crippling marathons beloved by the 'Blister Brigade' or of trying to race round the Three Peaks in a better time than the other idiots (and I've done both in former days) but of walking through the mountains, with one or two like-minded companions, a general aim in view, but nothing too specific except perhaps to make sure you reach a good pub long before closing time. Translated abroad, this can mean all sorts of things; helping the Gujar shepherds drive their flocks down the valley to escape the first snows of autumn in the Kashmiri highlands; pausing for an evil brew of *chang* on a trail in Nepal or joining the annual 'Leaf Peepers' as they head out of Boston in their Caddys to catch the glory of New England in the Fall.

October opens up a whole new world like no other month. In the southern hemisphere, of course, it heralds spring, but that doesn't concern us here because it is to the autumnal quality of the month that I want to draw attention. All over the northern hemisphere it has attractions no other month can match, but in this short feature I would like to mention just three places which October makes magical.

I live on the edge of the Lake District, so you

can accuse me of being partisan when I say that no part of Britain is as glorious as the Lakes in October. The bracken has turned a deep russet and throughout the month the trees gradually acquire their autumn colourings; the copper of the great beeches, the flame red of the maples and the yellows, browns and golds of a dozen other species. In some years the process lengthens well into November, in others the leaves have scarcely started to turn when some autumnal gale blows up out of the west and strips the trees down to their bare branches. There may be only a few days in which to enjoy the golden Lakes.

In medieval times the Lake District was a landscape of bare fell and gaunt crag, with long low farmhouses crouched against the wind. The original forest had long gone and the trees we see now came much later. Oak, ash and birch were planted in Elizabethan times in Borrowdale to provide timber for the copper mines. In the eighteenth century hazel was introduced to southern Lakeland to join the indigenous oak for coppicing; a method of growing thin sticks of wood suitable for turning into charcoal. It was used in the important local industry of gunpowder manufacture. Then on top of all this, during the Regency and throughout the nineteenth

October gold is lost on a monochrome picture but at its best here on Helm Crag above Grasmere, a part of the Lakes particularly good for autumn colouring (Walt Unsworth).

century came the villas of the cotton masters and wool barons; *nouveaux riches* from Lancashire and Yorkshire, who planted exotic trees on their estates — mostly between Windermere and Grasmere.

So these are the places in which best to observe golden October in the Lakes. Fortunately, they lend themselves to easy walking and modest endeavour.

It was as a schoolboy, during the war, that I was first introduced to Borrowdale by an enterprising teacher who would take us on Youth Hostel tours during the holidays. I always felt this valley had some special magic about it, which the others didn't have. It is ridiculously romantic, extremely beautiful; the ultimate expression of the perfect landscape. Looking up the valley from Friar's Crag on Derwentwater, John Ruskin declared it to be one of the three most beautiful views in Europe — leaving everyone to wonder what the other two were.

The valley has the three essential ingredients

Right *Dunmail Raise from Loughrigg Fell* (Walt Unsworth).

Below *On the Old Toll Road in Borrowdale, with Castle Crag on the right* (Walt Unsworth).

Rydal Water from Loughrigg Fell (Walt Unsworth).

of classical landscape: water, rocks and woods. The rocks peep through the trees and both are reflected in the water. It is superb scenery at any time of the year, even in deepest winter when the branches are bare and the rocks are streaked with snow, but in late autumn the browns and golds of the dying year give it an extra quality.

We were especially fond of what we called 'the Old Toll Road' in those early days; the broad track on the west side of the valley which runs from Grange to Honister, over the saddle between Castle Crag and Lobstone Band. The path goes through various woods before it bursts into the open on the fellside high above Rosthwaite, revealing in panoramic form the heart of the valley. The wooded dale of Stonethwaite funnels away towards Greenup Edge, with Heron Crag thrust out aggressively at the entrance to Langstrath. That superb fell, Glaramara, towers over all.

An October walk along the Old Toll Road is one of the great delights of Lakeland walking. Similarly, the walk along Loughrigg Terrace above the lake of Grasmere is equally rewarding and somewhat easier. It is best to start from Pelter Bridge on the Rothay and follow the pleasant path up the fellside above Rydal Water. There's a huge cave here — the remnant of old slate workings — filled with water and reminiscent of the Styx. As you stand on a ledge in the dark interior, listening to the lap-lap of the water, you wonder whether the Ferryman is coming.

The terrace runs a level course above Grasmere. Wooded promontories give the lake form and in the distance Helm Crag is reflected in the still waters. The village itself is invisible; you can't see the houses for the trees. If you are feeling energetic there's a direct route up Loughrigg Fell from the end of the terrace. It was until recently a badly eroded path but

Right *Langdale Pikes from Loughrigg* (Walt Unsworth).

Far right *Mount Mansfield is the highest of the Green Mountain summits. It is completely rocky and laced with a variety of trails similar to this one* (Walt Unsworth).

now it has been improved — and I use the word loosely — by fitting it with wooden steps. Perhaps the National Park authorities thought they were building a stairway to heaven! What they have done is construct the perfect example of how *not* to restore a mountain path.

Some time later they made amends with the path they built up Helm Crag to replace the one being destroyed there by human erosion. The new path is not only in harmony with its surroundings but it also takes a better line than the original. Like Loughrigg, it is worth climbing in October for the quality of the foliage. In fact, almost any of the short walks in the Ambleside-Grasmere area shows off Lakeland autumn at its best.

The people of Vermont, in New England on the eastern seaboard of the USA, have a dry sense of humour which they love to exercise at the expense of city slickers, especially those from New York.

'How do I get across this muddy road?' cried the well dressed New Yorker across the street in Brandon.

'Can't rightly say,' answers the local.

'Well, how the hell did you get across?' cried the New Yorker, exasperated.

'I was born on this side,' said the local.

Vermont is not at all like the popular misconception of the USA. It is Hicksville; but a very nice, kind Hicksville where the people are gentle and neighbourly and still very much in the mould portrayed on a thousand *Saturday Evening Post* covers by Norman Rockwell. Their forefathers were the Green Mountain Boys of Ethan Allen who fought the Indians and the French and surprised the British garrison at Fort Ticonderoga, forcing them to surrender ignominiously. It is, of course, archetypal New England with trim little towns in white clapboard, centred round the church and the inn. Manchester in Vermont is not a bit like its English namesake! The inns are justly famous for their food and hospitality; real family run concerns, often in eighteenth

century buildings, and a pleasant contrast to the Hiltons and Holiday Inns, which seem to be everywhere. But Vermont is like that — you won't, for instance, see any roadside advertising in this state, and they are pretty hot on litter, too.

It is a state of contrasts, most of which are not readily apparent. On the one hand it plays host to some of the most exclusive colleges in America, like Bennington, and has some of the poshest ski resorts, like Stowe, where the Von Trapps of *Sound of Music* fame, ended up. (When I was there a few years ago Maria was still running the hotel.) On the other hand it is one of the poorest states in the union, being mostly hills, trees and water.

'Can I take this road to New York?' asks the city slicker.

'Don't see why not — you've taken most everything else there,' replies the Vermonter.

In October, round about Halloween, the city folk in their thousands head out from New York and Boston to see the wonderful change which comes over the trees. The locals call them the 'Leaf Peepers', and accommodation in Vermont is at a premium.

Vermont calls itself 'the Green Mountain State' on account of the long range of tree clad hills which runs right through the state to the Canadian border. It is said that Vermont is a corruption of Vert Mont — with a stretch of credulity you could take that as pidgin French for Green Mountain. In summer the mountains are green, and a fairly dull green at that, but in October they shade to brown and there is a hint of change, then suddenly *wham*! the whole place turns red and gold in a glorious riot of colour. At its brilliant best it lasts only a few days.

In 1910 some local outdoor enthusiasts, the Green Mountain Club, began to create the Long Trail, which follows the crest of the mountains all the way to Canada. Their custody of this long distance path is now enshrined in State legislation, and they have erected signposts and built bothys, but not too many of either. Because the trail is long — 260 miles — it is usually done in sections and there are more variants than in the Hampton Court maze.

The blanket of dense forest reaches to the very summits of most of the peaks. Maple, birch and alder are the home of chipmunks, porcupines and even the occasional bear. Here and there rocky coigns break through the trees to give the walker a vantage point from which to view the surroundings. Two mountains, however, shake clear of the trees entirely — Mount Mansfield (4,393 ft), the highest summit in the Green Mountains, and the Camel's Hump (4,083 ft). On these two peaks the trees give way to rocks and tundra.

A friend and I walked these peaks one glorious October. On Mansfield the day was a bit drear and the mountain itself is disfigured by a radio station, not to mention a café which serves the worst coffee in America. We drove up to the station. The joy of Mansfield lies not in climbing the mountain but exploring the numerous variants to the Long Trail which criss-cross it in all directions. Mostly they are rocky and some have the qualities of a *via ferrata* in that iron ladders and handrails are needed from time to time, though they are nothing like as sensational as their Dolomite counterparts.

It was wonderful walking, with exhilarating views out over a carpet of red and gold to the distant peaks like Mt Ethan Allen, Deer Leap and Camel's Hump. We descended by the ordinary route and climbed back up by the Wampahoofus Trail — intrigued by the name, though I still have no idea what a Wampahoofus is or was. Further along we came to another curious variant called Subway, which starts and ends almost at the same place — a circular tour of the mountain's west face. This was a bit tougher than the rest, a sort of Mansfield Jack's Rake, which got its name because at one point it plunges underground.

It was a good fun day and as my friend and I stood on the summit we met a mother and daughter who had struggled bravely to the top from the car park, and later a couple of husky youths who seemed strong enough for anything. Fresh with enthusiasm I advised them all to take in Subway on the way back. As we waved them goodbye my friend expressed concern. 'I do wish you would stop sending people to their death,' he said.

The Camel's Hump was a different sort of mountain altogether: a straightforward climb up a delectable peak. As its name suggests it is a distinctive looking mountain, though it was in fact first called Camel's Rump, until the Vermonters of Victorian times thought the name was not polite enough for genteel conversation. It is a hump-shaped or bell-shaped peak standing at the end of a less spectacular approach ridge. The Long Trail traverses the ridge and the peak in one of its finest sections.

We approached the mountain from the Forest Service car park at Couching Lion farm. From here a number of trails lead through the woods to the summit, the shortest taking about three hours. However, our intention was to traverse the peak along the Long Trail and return by the 'ordinary' route. Experience had taught us that the side trails were usually well marked, so we had no fear of losing our way in the forest. The surprising thing is that the main trail is hardly marked at all, and I can assure you it is no joke being lost in a Vermont wood!

A recent trip up Deer Leap Mountain had familiarized us with the strange quality of the forest trails, though fresh acquaintance caused momentary surprise. The all-enveloping nature of it was so different from the openness of our British hills that it required a mental adjustment each time. Were we moving forward or standing still? In these woods it was hard to tell. We could walk for two hours and at the end of it the immediate surroundings were exactly the same as when we started.

On the Camel's Hump, however, the approach walk was a steady climb to the crest of the ridge so we knew we were getting somewhere and at last we came to a saddle with a clearing in which a log cabin had been built. We ate lunch then set off up the Long Trail towards the peak. It was a tiring climb and at the top of the ridge, the forerunner of the Hump, we flopped down on a rock glacis and looked about us. There was a clearing in the trees at this point and the edge of the glacis ended in a vertical cliff which plunged two or three hundred feet into beaver ponds

Climbing through the thick woods towards the Camel's Hump. This is typical of the Long Trail, which stretches all the way to the Canadian border — one of the earliest long distance footpaths in North America begun in 1910 (Walt Unsworth).

below. Beyond we could see the carpet of forest through which we had walked that morning and on either hand, the long range of summits that were the Green Mountains — except that, since it was the fall, a more appropriate name would have been Golden Mountains. They must have been named in springtime.

The final peak of Camel's Hump reared above us, fairly formidable. It seemed sheer rock on this side, but we were comforted by the knowledge that somehow the Long Trail traversed it, though just how was not immediately apparent. Expectation and a frisson of excitement entered our feelings. Before long we found ourselves scrambling up broken rock to the foot of the final tower. Here, hidden until the last moment, a narrow trail wound round the base of the crag to the left, then by easy cracks and slabs led to the very summit. The whole world lay below us. Mile upon mile of October splendour.

The Lakes and New England in October have the sweet softness of a good Sauterne. You can eat well in both places, sleep comfortably, and trim the exercise to fit the mood. That is not the case in other places. There is some October walking which has the sharp, dry sparkle of champagne. And like champagne, it can go to your head.

Nepal is a case in point. In post-monsoon October, before the bitter winds of winter make life too uncomfortable, the Himalayan air has an unbelievable clarity. Pin-sharp vision for miles and miles, peak piled upon peak in glorious array. In a mountaineer's October, it seems like Shangri La.

I first became acquainted with it back in

Everest from the trekkers' route up Kala Pattar with one of Nuptse's ridges in the foreground. Everest's south-west face is visible in detail, the north face stretches away to the left (Walt Unsworth).

1975 when I went to meet Bonington's party at Everest Base Camp, on their successful South-west Face expedition. As luck would have it they were ahead of schedule and we met at a party in the British Embassy in Kathmandu instead! However, I had no intention of being cheated out of a trip up the Khumbu, so with some comrades I did the time-honoured trek to Kala Pattar.

The trek has been described in numerous books and magazines, so I need hardly go into detail here as to the route. Suffice to say it begins at the airstrip at Lukla and follows a good trail up the Khumbu river to the Khumbu Glacier on the border with Tibet. Around the Khumbu are ranged some of the greatest mountains in the world: Everest, Lhotse, Nuptse, Pumori, Ama Dablam, Kangtega and many more. They are so near and so big that you feel you can reach out and touch them.

Autumn shows only in the valleys. There are no red maples here, but there is the berberis, prickly, red in leaf and berry, forming bloody patches on the bare hillsides. Sherpanis scratch the season's potato crop from the small cultivated strips near the villages while old Chumbi of Khumjung prepares his yaks for a trip over into Tibet, carrying plastic buckets for sale. He looks like an elderly Sherpa whose horizons have always been limited by the Khumbu mountains; kindly, old fashioned and distinctly scruffy compared with his modern counterparts — but Chumbi is no stranger to the world at large. He has been to Europe and America, showing off the yeti scalp from the local monastery to scientific bodies, who universally condemned it as a fake. Chumbi seems to have taken the rebuff philosophically. Asked about his preferences, he said he liked Chicago best.

It is the vignettes which make any trip memorable. We flew into Lukla in a private plane piloted by a 'Nam veteran listening to the radio telling him that 'Lukla is still open', as the clouds began to pile up over the mountains. Lukla is often closed for days on end, leaving hundreds of trekkers stranded. 'Can't you fly through cloud?' I asked the

Left *Chumbi — his horizons seem limited by his local mountains, but he has travelled widely in Britain and America* (Walt Unsworth).

pilot innocently.

'Yeah, but in Nepal the clouds sometimes have rocks inside,' he replied laconically. We swooped into Lukla like a kestrel after a vole. The airfield is a grass patch perched on the edge of all things, and the pilot has just one chance to make good. The edge of the field is littered with the wreckage of aircraft which failed the test.

At Jorsale a group of yellow-robed monks were rebuilding a bridge which had been swept away by the monsoons. I wondered if this sort of thing went on in the Yorkshire Dales during the Middle Ages, with monks from Fountains Abbey providing labour battalions. One monk was obviously the clerk-of-works; he directed everyone's efforts without doing much himself.

The famous monastery at Thyangboche has a large flat camping ground from which you catch a first glimpse of Everest. The setting is idyllic; an oasis in a wilderness of blue and white mountain spires. It is getting fairly high here — not quite 13,000 ft — and for the first

time you have the sobering thought that there is still another 6,000 ft to go, more or less. I had this thought reinforced in an unpleasant way when I discovered that the rolled up tent next to mine contained the body of a Swedish trekker who had succumbed to pulmonary oedema. Slowly, slowly, catchee monkey is definitely the rule of the road in the Khumbu.

Pulmonary and cerebral oedema, the two fatal forms of altitude sickness, are very democratic afflictions in that they strike at anybody irrespective of age, sex, fitness or anything else, as far as is known. At least one Alpine guide has died from it on the Everest trek, whereas quite a number of trekkers, far into their October years, have not been affected at all. A slow ascent, with days out to acclimatize, is the best preventative. We took days off in Namche, Thyangboche and Pheriche. Even so, one of our number decided to go no higher than Pheriche — a cruel blow when Everest is so near. A few years ago the death rate from oedema on the Everest trek was about twelve people per year. The

In the Dudh Kosi valley near Lukla. This is the start of the long trek to the base of Everest (Walt Unsworth).

Himalayan death rate for climbers and trekkers combined, and for all causes, is reputed to be ten per cent. One in ten don't make it? It's a sobering thought.

But it is not a thought you think whilst you are there. Life is too good for that. The going may be hard, the sleeping even harder, and the food pretty revolting, but there is that champagne sparkle to the whole affair. At the end of the valley we camped for the night on the moraines near Gorak Shep, a glacial tarn. It was 17,000 ft and cold at night. Next day we toiled up the boulder slopes of Kala Pattar while the great peak of Pumori towered overhead. Kala Pattar is one of Pumori's lesser satellites and the top is 18,450 ft — a little

further and you could actually tackle the first ice-encrusted gendarme of the south ridge! That was very far from my thoughts as I panted up the last slopes to the top, wondering whether this was my physical limit.

Peak piles on peak in an astonishing view from Kala Pattar. Ama Dablam, whose perfection of form makes it every child's vision of a mountain, dominates the distance but nearer at hand is the beautiful Nuptse (25,851 ft), all fluted ice and formidable ridges. And Everest itself, not a beautiful mountain, and in a strange way, not particularly dominating, but *there* — as Mallory said. Gone was the tiredness, the shortage of breath. What a way to spend October.

The final climb to reach the summit of Kala Pattar is within the capabilities of most trekkers. In the background is the Kangtega group (Walt Unsworth).

'Every child's vision of a mountain' — Ama Dablam is but one of many superb peaks on the Everest trek (Walt Unsworth).

A magnificent peak of ice flutings and savage ridges — Nuptse is the incredible sight that greets trekkers from Kala Pattar (Walt Unsworth).

Walt Unsworth was born in the shadow of the Pennine hills and has spent a lifetime looking beyond the last blue mountain; walking and climbing in many parts of the world. *Classic Walks of the World* and *Savage Snows* are two of his recent books: one reflecting his interest in topography and the other in mountain history. One of Britain's leading mountain writers, he is also Editorial Director of Cicerone Press, the well-known guide-book company, and Executive Editor of *Climber* magazine.

The Quantocks of November

BRIAN ATKIN

Traffic streams continuously all day and for much of the night along the motorway running westwards from London. Having left the metropolis and its extensive suburbs, those travellers who care to look about them, will see mile upon mile of typical lowland English countryside. Neat farms, hedgerows and copses are set upon a succession of very gentle hills and valleys.

However, there is one exception just before the gradual descent from the chalk ridge near Swindon. For a brief moment the stark outline of a hill crowned by a small clump of trees known as Liddington Castle looms on the left hand side. November adds bleakness to the aura of sadness which pervades this place even on a summer's day. The hill is one of several claimed to be the site of Mount Badon where King Arthur inflicted a crushing defeat on the Anglo Saxons and thereby halted their westward advance for more than a generation. The facts are true but the site in doubt. The one certain thing is the presence of the massive Iron Age hill fort on its summit, one of many strung out along the chalk escarpment like a prehistoric Maginot Line providing mute evidence of long forgotten troubles. This was the place where I came off the hill one memorable sunny evening footsore, thirsty and very happy at the end of the first stage of the Ridgeway Path from Avebury.

After Swindon the scenery continues much as before. There is a higher proportion of pasture, although by November many of the familiar black and white Friesian cattle are out of sight in their cowsheds. The major change though, occurs after Bristol. Here the motorway swings southwards roughly parallel to the shore of the nascent Severn Estuary, soon to grow into the Bristol Channel. The previous wide spaces of soft gentle landscape are replaced by a harder one made of ancient rocks. Being born and brought up a lowlander may have something to do with it, but no matter how many times I return to upland Britain I have a feeling of suppressed

excitement at the boundary between new and old. The sight of wild and often rugged scenery, the aura of great age, remoteness and an elusive air of mystery are all components of the explanation.

Even where the motorway breaks out onto the Somerset Levels my mood does not change. Unlike the fens and sea marshes of the East where the eye continually seeks out any small projection above the flat, the surrounding Somerset hills always dominate. First there are the mountain limestones of the Mendips. The elegant inappropriately named Crook Peak bears rock outcrops on its sides reminiscent of my much loved White Peak and Craven Dales. These are followed by the striking isolated mound of Brent Knoll. At this point on the journey a long ridge of hills has become apparent hull down in the distance across the levels as if to block the way ahead. These are the Quantocks. After this first sighting I can barely wait to arrive. At the first opportunity I abandon my car (which is merely a convenient means of transport from one walking area to another) put on my boots and find myself bounding up the nearest hill.

The time–span may seem less but it is now over 35 years since I first walked on these hills. My friend and I had spent the night in Taunton and we came up the following morning by bus. I can no longer remember where our walk started but Bagborough Hill seems to fit the place. However, the memory of the subsequent glorious autumn ramble in sun and showers along the ridge to finish above the Bristol Channel at West Quantoxhead remains as fresh as it was on that first day.

The satisfying shape of the Quantocks, their apparent wildness, the variety of bright colours of gorse, ripened grass, bracken and heather and the sparkling sea made so deep an impression that they immediately became my favourite hills. We then went on to Exmoor. Such is fickle human nature that the new hills and especially their coast soon supplanted the

Right *The author and his dog on the top* (Brian Atkin).

Top right *St Audries Bay is a place to walk, look and admire: a place where the shore and sea meet in dramatic conjunction* (Brian Atkin).

Bottom right *Another view of St Audries Bay clearly shows the dramatic rock formations and the large area of beach exposed at low tide* (Brian Atkin).

Quantocks from their prime position. As things turned out I did not return to the Quantocks for many years although they were often in my thoughts. Recently I have had great pleasure in re-making their acquaintance and in getting to know them well.

Although the Quantocks are hills for enjoyment at all seasons their unique qualities make them particularly appropriate for winter walking. Much of this pleasure lies in their size, shape and surface features which can be best appreciated by some knowledge of underlying geology. The long whale-backed ridge is made up of three ancient types of sedimentary rocks which are set in a south-east/north-west alignment. All the rocks are approximately 400 million years old but the hardest, oldest and most resistant, which are known by the colourful name of Hangman Grits, occur at their northern end which is also the seaward extremity. These are followed by the Ilfracombe Beds and Morte slates.

Those familiar with the North Devon coast to the west of the Quantocks will recognize the names. It was in these coastal locations that the types of rocks were first identified and classified. The old rocks of the Quantocks were later surrounded by younger ones composed of New Red Sandstone and Lias, the latter being a type of grey-blue limestone. These are also sedimentary in type and I have read somewhere that the New Red Sandstone was laid down in a shallow sea at a time when the Quantocks were an island.

Though now in a much worn down condition the hills still give the impression of an island — standing above the lower countryside around. Long term erosion by rain, snow and temperature change have softened their shape. The ice caps of the last Ice Age did not reach this far south, so the extensive mountain sculpture which took place 10,000 years ago, and is today exemplified by the Lake District, cannot be seen here. Instead the Quantocks' rock mass tilts up towards the south-west where an eroded scarp drops steeply down to lower land, in contrast to the more gentle slopes facing the north-east. At

first glance the eye notes the mass of the ridge and soft rounded tops. Only then does it pass on to the most distinctive feature of the hills, the deep combes in their sides. These have been produced over millions of years by the erosion of rainwater and melted snow draining down from the tops. The combes facing the south-west are short, steep and dramatic:those on the opposite side are long and winding, but equally beautiful.

From the north, which is often the newcomer's first view, the hills appear to be well wooded. This impression is created by a combination of extensive new coniferous forest which lies on the eastern flanks together with some older deciduous woodlands further to the north. Closer inspection soon reveals that much of the higher ground is open moorland. Here exposed weather conditions and poor acid soil only allow growth of limited species such as heather, gorse, bracken, whortleberry and wiry grass. Rhododendron, a relative newcomer, is also becoming established in some parts. On the tops there is no ridge, but a wide plateau crowned at intervals by low summits. In this respect the Quantocks are similar to the extensive tops of nearby Dartmoor and Exmoor but the quagmires and bogs of the last two are not to be found here. The ground is almost always

firm underfoot and the pools which do exist are few and well spaced. In summer they provide much needed drinking water for animals.

There may be a wayfinding problem in poor visibility and use of a compass is sometimes necessary. This is not due to a dearth of tracks and paths across the moor but rather to their multiplicity. On closer inspection each apparent slight hollow in the plateau turns out to be the head of one of the combes. Here scattered small weatherbeaten thorns, rowans and occasional hollies struggle for a meagre existence. Only a short distance below, the valley has dropped steeply downhill between high banks. Sparse scrub is replaced by sessile oaks which soon become big and tall. The abrupt change from open moorland to dense forest is quite dramatic, never more so than on a cold November day when a walker moving in the opposite direction passes from near complete protection to total exposure in a few strides.

Autumn usually continues well into November in this mild country. The purple of the heather may be past its best but there is still sufficient colour to delight. The arrays of gold, red and yellow remain on many deciduous trees, but by month end winter has come and only a few obstinate leaves cling to the branches. Daylight now penetrates to deep places from which it has been banished for many months. The faded fallen colours lie in a thick carpet on the ground. For a short time they protect a walker passing through the bottoms of the combes from the newly formed mud beneath his feet.

When skies are clear night cools down rapidly to near freezing point. With the coming of day the sun, no longer wide ranging from the east but confined to the southern quarter, climbs only a short way into the sky before falling away. The hours of darkness are long and days seem little more than sunrises and sunsets. Yet the low zenith at midday can still manage to provide a brief warmth which collects in south facing nooks away from the wind to gladden the body and heart. Sun worship returns at this season: a few months earlier the shade of trees would have been more than welcome for respite. Then one would have heard nothing more than the tinkling brook and lazily watched butterflies and insects flitting through shafts of sunlight.

The change of season is less obvious in coniferous woodland because the trees remain verdant and so do the rhododendrons which colonize the brooksides. The Forestry Commission's Quantock Forest covers much of the central section of the dip slopes of these hills. Commercial softwoods are a controversial and often intrusive feature in Britain's upland scenery due to insensitive planting without regard to terrain and existing flora. However, the Quantock Forest is attractive because the trees which were mostly planted sixty years ago have now reached majestic proportions and elsewhere hardwoods have been retained and planted in some of the more visible parts of the forest. The conifers range over a series of combe bottoms, sides and intervening hill spurs rising up towards the main plateau crest. There are some open spaces where old trees have been felled and forest tracks and bridleways are to be found everywhere.

Unlike many of the hardwoods, these conifer forests are not native to our part of the world

Winter afternoon on the Quantock tops (Brian Atkin).

and for this reason always seem somewhat alien. Whenever I come upon one I am reminded not of home but of holidays in far flung places ranging from North America, Scandinavia, the Balkans and even Corsica and Tenerife. The Quantock forest adds a pleasurable third dimension to those of moorland top and hardwood. However, I would not wish to see a greater coverage of these hills, because the underlying unnatural uniformity and lack of birds and other wildlife are very obvious.

November brings more solitude to the hills and even in the fretting winds there is a new peace. Now the lone walker on the tops far away from his fellows senses contact and even companionship with the past. This region of England may be a little removed from those where kings, chiefs and their supporters determined the destiny of our nation but ordinary folk have lived here since the first hunters came this way.

As in many parts of the country the Celtic and pre-Celtic past are only just below the surface of an Anglo Saxon crust. The name

'Quantock' is believed to be a derivation of the Celtic word 'gwantog' which, appropriately, means a place full of combes. There is a possible poignant connection with the past in the name of the Quantocks' highest hill, Wills Neck (1,260 ft). This is not Celtic but Anglo Saxon. Will is derived from the Germanic word 'Wealas' which is contained in Wales, Cornwall and Walloon and means 'foreigner'. The word 'nek' means ridge: thus 'foreigners ridge'. A prominent hill standing out from the scarp of the Quantocks may have still been the fort of a Celtic community some time after the surrounding fertile lowlands had been settled by incomers.

More tangible memorials to the past include the remains of Bronze Age tumuli on or near the higher points of many of the hills. There are also some very substantial Iron Age hill forts including my favourite, Dowsborough. Its ramparts crown a prominent and graceful wooded hill overlooking the nearby deep Holford Combe and the more distant low country away to the east. However, the most important survival from prehistoric times is the ridgeway which runs the length of the Quantocks from the Vale of Taunton Deane and probably from much further afield down to the sea at, or near, modern Watchet. This way was old long before the Iron Age forts were built and long before the present day roads below the hill, which now carry all the traffic, had been hacked through natural forest.

The solitary wayfarer marching along the ridgeway as it passes over wide moor and between lines of trees senses a real bond with the past. This link may have something to do with simultaneously moving along the dimensions of time and distance, a combination not possible if one merely goes to look at an ancient site. An alternative and more likely explanation is that he is doing exactly the same as countless people who came along this way before him, albeit less well shod and more heavily laden!

On most days in November only the presence of sheep is obvious although one or two small groups of ponies and perhaps a solitary rider may be seen from time to time. Wildlife and deer are also there but will be invisible if the wind blows strong and cold. The deer are probably not wildlife in the strict sense of the word because they were introduced or perhaps reintroduced to these hills by man for the purpose of hunting about

Top left *Holford Combe is typical of the numerous small valleys running off the tops* (Brian Atkin).

Bottom left *Small streams through the combes (this is Holford Combe again) quickly rise in wet winter weather but rarely present a major obstacle to the walker* (Brian Atkin).

Cattle in winter sunshine: the Ridgway is on the skyline (Brian Atkin).

a hundred and fifty years ago. These graceful animals live mostly in the combes but can be seen at their best when venturing out on to the tops to forage for food. It is not possible to get close to them because they are very shy of humans — with very good reason.

To come up on the hills seeking familiar peace and pleasure and by chance find oneself surrounded by the activities of a hunt is a shattering experience. Where the only sound should be that of sighing wind and the only movements those of clouds, sea and waving grass, there is a noisy melée of huntsmen and huntswomen, their horses and hounds. A large

collection of horse transporters and vehicles driven by the hunt followers tear along the moorland tracks. Raucous excitement is everywhere.

I recognize that the individual may have to kill for food and be prepared to fight and kill for survival or to protect family or country. However, I consider that to do so in a barbarous fashion for mere pleasure is distasteful in the extreme. The deer on the hill have no natural predators and, therefore, some form of cull is necessary in order to control numbers. However, there must be a better way of carrying it out than in the painful and distressing manner in which these animals are literally hounded to death. Obviously, the hunters and I share a pleasure in these wild places but beyond that we have nothing in common. They go their way and I go mine — which means that I avoid them as much as possible.

Other developments were taking place about the time deer hunting was being introduced to the Quantocks. The hills of our country were becoming an attraction to a new group of people who walked for pleasure. Towards the end of the 18th century attitudes to wild places began to change. In previous times when the efforts of most people were totally committed to mere survival, they had been regarded as unprofitable wastes unworthy of consideration. Now, for the first time, hills and mountains were being seen for their interest, beauty and romanticism. Amongst the first of these new walkers on the Quantocks were William and Dorothy Wordsworth. The brother and sister, attracted to the area by their friend Coleridge, already established in Nether Stowey, rented a substantial house close to Holford at the foot of the hills and not far from the sea.

In this modern age nobody would pay any attention to a couple extolling the scenery as they walked over the hills and along the shore. They might not even attract too much attention if observed to be composing poetry. But to the simple country folk of that period their behaviour was incomprehensible and therefore foreign. Since the Napoleonic Wars were in progress at the time the locals, by their own straightforward logic, concluded that William and Mary must be French spies. It is said that the antagonism arising from this conjecture led to their early departure from the area.

On returning to Cumbria William entered his most successful period of poetry making and although best known for their Lake District associations, they clearly had a great affection for the Quantocks, feelings which many others have shared since. The beauty of the tops is only surpassed by the distant views that they offer. To the west the ground drops sharply to a patchwork of woods, small fields and villages nearly 1,000 ft below. This is the archetypal English countryside of the imagination rather than the reality of modern industrial farming. The scene is reminiscent of youthful rambles through farms which, although hundreds of years old, still gave the impression of having

been wrought by hand one field at a time from the primaeval forest.

The nearest hills to the Quantocks lie beyond this farmland. These are the Brendons. Although of similar height they are, by comparison, much more tamed with little moorland evident today. However, closer inspection reveals extensive scars of iron workings along their tops. The height of this activity took place during the second half of the 19th century when a remarkable mineral railway incorporating a long steep incline was constructed to carry the ore down to Watchet. On arrival the trucks were trundled out onto the quay and their contents offloaded into sailing vessels en route for the iron works in Ebbw Vale.

One recent sunny summer afternoon I met an elderly man on top of St Decuman's Church tower at Watchet. He caught my attention by his upright bearing in spite of age, the fact that he had managed to climb the extremely steep and dark spiral staircase and the remarkable polish of his light brown boots. We drifted into conversation in the typical fashion of strangers at a viewpoint. However, I noticed that his eyes were concentrating on the Brendons and not on either the sea or the nearer and to my mind, much more attractive Quantocks. He went on to talk of the iron workings during which he observed that the old iron masters should have been obliged to have built their smelting works here rather than carry the ore over the sea to Wales. At the time I was only conscious of the transferred regret of an earlier generation in his words about loss of potential job opportunities. When I next climbed Beacon Hill, the most prominent high point on the northern end of the Quantocks, the full implication of his words struck home. If those earlier hopes had been fulfilled this hill would now overlook the very visible remains of an abandoned steelworks and a decaying largish town rather than the reality of a small and relatively prosperous little port set in a rural scene.

However, some very visible modern industrial structures do exist a few miles away to the north-east. They are large and bulky with sharp lines and angles contrasting uncompromisingly with the gentle curves of nature. Though not an eyesore, their intrusive presence induces a conscious feeling of doubt and unease when all around speaks of the familiar pleasures of the countryside. These structures are the reactors and generator buildings of Hinkley Point nuclear power station.

Towards the east the ground falls away gradually to the Somerset Levels. These flat lands are always sombre, especially in winter, as if to remind us that in former times they would have been a watery waste, neither land nor sea at this season. It was here in the summer of 1685 that countryfolk rebels armed with pitchforks fought for their non-conformist religion under the charismatic Duke of Monmouth and were decimated by the professional army of his uncle the Roman Catholic King James II. Many of the rebels would have come over the Quantocks on their way to the Battle of Sedgemoor.

During the subsequent severe repression others were brought back to their home villages at the foot of the hills for execution in the horrific fashion of the times. This was the last major pitched battle in England. The irony is that their sacrifice proved unnecessary because the King was deposed a short time later and replaced by the Dutch protestant, William. It is said that the scars of the traumatic battle and aftermath were evident in West Somerset for many subsequent generations. After this brief terrible event the West Country has never again taken a direct hand in national affairs.

To the south the Quantocks glide down to the Vale of Taunton Deane backed by the gentle Blackdown Hills. Further away and usually out of sight are the wide moors and impressive granite outcrops of Dartmoor. Beyond them lies another southern sea. Exmoor stands along the western horizon with Dunkery Beacon rising above the rest. This region with its magnificent coast and empty spaces is another land of delight. On approach the Quantocks may seem to be a barrier. Certainly modern roads detour away from them, but for me these hills will always represent the gateway to the wonders of the south-west and their beauty a foretaste of much more to come.

Whilst on the subject of views, my wife and I enjoyed an exceptional experience one late

Descending into Bicknoffer Combe (Brian Atkin).

November day. We had set out early from London in darkness and fog, doubting the wisdom of our journey, and eventually arrived at Crowcombe Combe Gate on top of the Quantocks around mid-morning. Here for the first time we were reassured because the sky had started to lighten and the sun showed some signs of breaking through. So it did, even before we left the rough very wet grass hillside above the entrance to the forest in Rams Combe. As we ambled on the sun came and went, alternately a shrouded yellow globe and then missing as patches of mist drifted down through the trees. Sometimes the valley tops and brightening sky were visible through serried ranks of tall straight trunks and at others only nearby trees and damp grey were visible.

By the time we had looped around and come out above Keepers Combe the views of the tree clad heights above Rams Combe and Cockercombe were sharp and clear in bright sunlight. The sky above might have been an icy bright blue, traced with a thin wisp of high cloud, but the air about us was as still and warm as on a summer day. The mist had all gone.

Therefore, we were unprepared for the surprise which awaited us on the ridge at Triscombe stone. Instead of the extensive views over land to the south and west we were confronted by a sea of billiant gossamer

Right *The way down to Rams Combe can be muddy underfoot on a November morning* (Brian Atkin).

Far right *Beyond Wilmots Pool, part of which may be seen in the foreground, can be seen a blustery Bristol Channel* (Brian Atkin).

white which reached up the hill almost to our feet. Nearby the summit of Wills Neck, black against the sun, rose from this dazzling mass. Far away a small unrecognizable part of distant Exmoor was briefly visible before it too went away. That was all, none of the usual multitude of features were to be seen from this place, no land, no sea, nothing.

The sight could be likened to that from an aeroplane at around 15,000 ft. Once again the Quantocks were performing their familiar illusion of being much grander than reality should suggest. The view did not last for long. The earlier stillness in the valleys and trees had been replaced by a small cool breeze blowing up the slope. in no time at all this brought the mist back up the hill and we were engulfed by cold and damp. The best of this magic winter's day was already over and it was still only two o'clock.

In normal circumstances the best view from the Quantocks ranges from west via north to north-east. The sea is the dominant feature in this sector. All those born and brought up on the coast share the same lifetime affinity and respect for the sea. No scene without it, no matter how beautiful, is ever quite complete. My own native shore with its low-lying villages clinging under the lea of fragile sand dunes for protection from a sullen North Sea is very far removed from this Somerset scene, but the sea is always the sea, no matter where. Part of the attraction lies in the sharp boundary between extreme contrasts; on one side the complex variety of hills, fields, trees, roads, houses, people and all the paraphernalia of thousands of years of civilization and on the other a flat emptiness where the moods of nature are paramount and where man cannot venture on his own terms. There is also an excitement that the same sea, far removed from our temperate island, laps round all the world's shores from lands icy and strange to hot and exotic.

The Quantocks stand high above the sea at their northern end. On one side the Channel can be seen gradually dwindling to the Severn Estuary and on the other broadening out into the wide Atlantic. Western gales, dark skies and white crested muddy waters are usually associated with November but the sea at this time can still be a huge mill pond reflecting a deeper blue than the sky above. These two massive splashes of colour can dominate when all other autumn hues have faded or are gone. The faces of the sea are infinite ... dappled waters and cloud shadows on windy days, sullenness under heavy clouds, little or no sea at all when the mists roll in ...

The Bristol Channel at this point is only fifteen miles wide. On clear days every detail on the Welsh shore is visible and far beyond the outlines of hills and mountains are sharp and clear. When the early winter nights close in, the land across the water comes closer and twinkling lights of town and countryside appear to be on the other side of a broad river. Yet when there is a slight haze over the sea the waters seem to stretch out from the Somerset

shore to infinity.

One eye-catching feature of the seascape is the island of Steep Holm which lies in the middle of the Channel between Weston-Super-Mare and Penarth. This is a half mile long cliff-girt hump on the sea. It is geologically a piece of Mendip limestone which has somehow become detached from the parent range. There is also a Flat Holm which is much less obvious, partly for the reason suggested by its name and partly for a propensity to lurk behind the taller neighbour. Sometimes Steep Holm appears as the island it is and at other times as a large vessel moored in the sea. On rare occasions when a very light breeze only slightly ruffles some stretches of intervening water it can

appear as a balloon floating in the sky.

I am one of those people who is a compulsive map reader. Every line and feature contains something of interest and grounds for speculation. I remember old walks and plan out new ones both practical and fantastic. Names also tell a great deal. It so happens that my family origins are in the heart of the old Danelaw and I tend to cast around any map for homely words bearing the suffix of -by or -toft, -thorpe, -ness, -beck, -holm ... Suddenly, right in the middle of a map of lands around the Bristol Channel full of Anglo Saxon and Celtic names, two isolated Danish 'Holms' leapt out before my eyes.

Unfortunately the Danes do not have a good

record in the Quantock region. The earliest annals of nearby Watchet commence with rapes, robberies and murders carried out by the Danes and the present day citizens plan to celebrate the first millenia of these events with great gusto in the near future. The town's very local saint, St Decuman, was beheaded by the Danes. Things were not as bad as they might seem because he washed his head in a spring and then placed it back on his body! Some doubt may exist about the truth of this tale, but the spring, well tended and signposted, is authentic enough and can still be seen to this day.

Steep Holm seems to have been the Danes' strategic base from which they mounted their forays. Accounts say it was also the place to which they retreated after a major defeat and where many of the battle survivors subsequently starved. There is some confusion about the number and extent of defeats these warriors suffered but by tradition they appear to have been numerous and probably didn't have everything their own way. Curiously several local hills seem to have been involved in a rather similar pattern of setbacks including Dowsborough, that favourite of mine which is also known as Danesborough. I console myself with the thought that even today losers do tend to get an undeservedly bad press.

Although the Quantocks drop steeply to the sea, the cliffs immediately below the end of the ridge are not composed of the ancient gritstone core. Here bands of younger blue grey lias are exposed and these change to red sandstone on the approach to St Audries Bay. I like Quantock's Head. The grey, near vertical cliffs look out on an extensive eroded rock platform of many miniature scarps and dips which twist and turn following the old rock convulsions. The seashore ridges are composed of bare rock. The intervening gullies contain seawater pools and seaweed at low tide. The lias fractures naturally into rectangular boulders and these too lie scattered in the rills and run-off channels.

The long tapering shape of the Bristol Channel has produced one of the world's largest tidal ranges and the extent of the foreshore rock wilderness is very considerable

The rock platform at Quantocks Head in a winter shower (Brian Atkin).

Right *From the beach at St Audries, Blue Ben and the end of the Quantocks mark the change from shore to moorland scenery* (Brian Atkin).

at low tide. Seashores are areas where neither the flora of the land nor that of the sea can properly establish themselves. The result is a sort of wet desert. Few people appear to come to Quantock's Head, which is always cool in summer and bitterly cold when the wind blows off the sea in November. A walk along the shore is an interesting challenge of navigation and sure-footedness. The walker progresses alternately rapidly and slowly, depending on whether the way ahead is along an apparently well paved causeway or over a series of sharp edged ridges and hollows.

At high tide the sea washes the foot of the cliff. A foreshore walker should check the state of tide because there are no escape routes between East Quantoxhead and St Audries. There is also no alternative route parallel to the shore. In former times the area was notorious for smugglers and it is highly probable that there was once a coastguard patrol path along the top of the cliffs. Although there are delightful high paths along the coast both east and west, none now exist along the five-mile section between East Quantoxhead and Watchet. This major omission from an otherwise comprehensive Quantock footpath network ought to be remedied by a tourist-conscious local authority.

Blue Ben, a rugged projection of cliff, marks the seaward extremity of the Quantocks. The same name also applied to a dragon once reputed to have lived in these parts. He was often ridden by the Devil during routine inspections of Hell. After these excursions the monster bathed in the sea to cool off. Unfortunately for the creature concerned, on one occasion he got so hot that he plunged into the water and drowned. The deserted atmosphere of this unusual place, the large coiled fossils in the rocks and strange hissing sounds emanating from interstices in the seashore strata lend credence to such stories of the supernatural.

Another dragon inhabited nearby Shervage Wood which stands below Dowsborough. Although this one went under the delightful name of Gurt Vurm, he was a typically nasty creature who had a habit of eating animals and people. His ignominious end came when an

unknowing woodman sat down on the Vurm for lunch, thinking he had found a comfortable log. The 'log' moved so the woodman jumped up and chopped it in two with his axe. That was the end of the Gurt Vurm.

These two tales are illustrative of the somewhat whimsical versions of legends which have come down to us. They probably date from a period when the stories had already lost much of their potency amongst the locals. One can sense that further back in time, when understanding of the natural world was rudimentary and superstitions held sway, these legends would have been a source of real fear and dread.

The rocky beach at this northern end is a suitable place to ponder on the Quantocks as a whole. They offer pleasure to all, especially the walker, because only he or she can seek out the beauty of all the hidden places. They also offer a unique haven for city dwellers who have managed to escape briefly from the clamour and pressures of modern urban society. Yet this one special corner of England is very small indeed, barely four miles in width and rather less than a dozen in length. It may be necessary to go further afield to enjoy long distance walks, but one does not usually have these in mind during the month of November. Appositely they are ideal for winter excursions when daylight hours are short and the weather more likely to turn unpleasant. Yet, unlike most small hills, these give the impression of being large, wild and lonely, whether one is wandering in the midst of their many secluded woodlands or above on the moorland plateau. The secret is that the nearby gentle countryside and surrounding villages are hidden away out of sight.

Life is a progression of cycles. The massive Channel tides ebb and flow, alternatively baring and covering the rocky foreshore. Successive short days are followed by longer and darkening nights. We think of November as the onset of winter, but once arrived it has soon gone. By the end of the month the low point of the year is only three weeks away. The coldest weather is yet to come but soon the days, very slowly at first, and then with increasing speed, lengthen towards spring with its promise of bright new greens and flowers

Left *The waterfall at St Audries Bay* (Brian Atkin).

A glimpse of the Quantocks from Watchet West pier (Brian Atkin).

to deck the hills. The cycle of seasons has begun again. The patterns of tide, day and seasons which make up each year repeat themselves endlessly but nothing is ever quite the same again. Life is made up of many separate moments. The fleeting turn of a deer, a soaring buzzard, wind waving through old grass, the contrast of bright light and shadow on opposite sides of tree trunks lit by a low sun, the rush of a brook, the burst of sunlight after a shower, the unforgettable plaintive cry of a solitary curlew, long misty rays of the sun piercing through a mass of tree trunks and the sudden sight of the silver sea over the brow of a hill, are all Quantock November moments which are forever.

Brian Atkin comes from an old East Lincolnshire farming family. A lifetime's walking, which began on the windy sandy beach of his home village, has led him far and wide. However, England, with its infinite variety of scenery and atmosphere of history, remains his firm favourite. Brian is a professional engineer with an adult family. He and his wife now live in London where his one regret is lack of time for more walking and writing.

The Dales of December

COLIN SPEAKMAN

W. H. Auden once said that there is a little bit of landscape in every one of us, a place with which we most closely identify ourselves, no matter how far we stray away from it. For me, I have to confess, that special landscape is the Yorkshire Dales.

It's an area which covers a good deal of our northern hill country, certainly far more than that which enjoys the protection, theoretical or otherwise, of being in the National Park. Its southern boundary is defined roughly by the Aire-Wharfe gap, north of the two trunk roads, the A59 and A65, which cut across from east to west. Its northern boundary is the Stainmore gap as defined by the A66/A68, with the M6 a natural frontier to the west, while the eastern boundary falls where the eastern foothills fade into the Plain of York and Vale of Mowbray, west of the towns of Ripon, Leyburn and Richmond.

If all that countryside was, as it should be, included in the National Park, it would make the Dales the largest of the ten Parks. In fact, the Park boundary is a nonsense, based on politics rather than landscape or geomorpholgy, designed to ensure that exactly the same acreage was given to each of the two old Yorkshire Counties, West Riding and North Riding, with Westmorland totally excluded. That's why half the Howgill Fells are outside the National Park, as well as such superlative areas as Wild Boar Fell, the Mallerstang valley, High Seat, Upper Nidderdale, the top of Colsterdale and much other beautiful countryside, as grand as anything in England.

What makes the Dales so very special for me is that you have this extraordinary blend of grandeur and intimacy. There are the fells which, in the west, have the status of mountains in every sense, most notably the 'Three Peaks' of Ingleborough, Whernside and Pen-y-Ghent, but also such superb summits as Gregareth, Wild Boar Fell, and High Seat. Further east there are superb areas of gritstone moorland, much of them heather covered, which east of Wharfedale, Nidderdale and Coverdale finally peter out into the foothills of the Pennines west of Masham, Ripon, and Harrogate.

This high fell country is penetrated by steep-sided valleys such as Dentdale, Swaledale, Langstrothdale and Coverdale whose beauty is essentially small scale, a human landscape of drystone-walled enclosures, farmhouses whose careful siting and traditional style go back a thousand years, scattered barns, meadows as

Tracing the course of a footpath through dormant trees on a bright December day is one of the winter pleasures of Wharfedale (Colin Speakman).

old as England, whole villages whose mellow limestone walls reflect nearby crags and escarpments so exactly that they seem to have grown out of the very soil.

It's as if, in the Dales, there's a special harmony established between man and nature, a compromise perhaps between the struggle to earn a living in a harsh climate and from thin soils and an acceptance that the wilderness is untameable. But the high fells covered with heather or rough moorland grasses, peat hags or semi-tundra are bleak, empty places, treeless, inhabited only by plant life and living creatures who have ruthlessly adapted for survival.

In geological terms the Dales have been carved by the action of glaciers and fast-flowing rivers out of a great high plateau, leaving enormous ridges, smooth topped, like gigantic beached whales, with the characteristic stepped edges on their western flank where the Yoredale limestone has weathered more slowly than softer shales. Wherever you are in the Dales, the fell tops are never far away. You look up and see the high skyline, dominating the valley so that, in winter months at least, houses on northern slopes are in almost perpetual shade. You know that only a few minutes' brisk walk from where you live, work or merely visit, you will be in a vast, empty landscape, all space, air and light, where human affairs are but triviality. That

knowledge adds a seriousness to human endeavours in the Dales. Dales people, for all their warmth and humour, are fundamentally serious people, in touch with realities. Little wonder that generations of Quakers and scholars have come from the Yorkshire Dales, serious-minded people who have often achieved great things, particularly in the sciences.

This is sheep farming country and the Swaledale or Dalesbred sheep, descendants of Viking and Monastic breeds, are among the toughest quadrupeds to walk this planet, able to endure and survive the worst of blizzards and deepest of snowdrifts. But for much of the year, when the wind comes straight off the sea or from the polar regions, the highest summits of the Dales are too much even for these superbly adapted beasts and you'll find the nearest thing in England to total solitude on those great, empty wastes, particularly on the eastern side of the Dales, between Wharfedale and Nidderdale, above Coverdale and Colsterdale — maybe the loneliest places in all England.

Perhaps because publishers so very often have early spring deadlines, I do a lot of walking in winter, particularly in December. But for anyone who loves the hills, December is both a frustrating and a fascinating month. The frustration lies in the fact that it is short. Not a shortage of days — there are 31 of those.

Left *Malhamdale offers the stark outlines of limestone scarps and pavements, scraped into being by a massive ice sheet, which, in geological terms, was here only yesterday* (Colin Speakman).

Below left *One of the attractions of the Dales is the rugged honesty of buildings such as this traditional farmhouse near Hatton Gill in Littondale* (Lydia Speakman).

Below *An occasional stubborn thorn tree, ravaged by countless winters, forces its way through a limestone pavement near Ingleborough* (Lydia Speakman).

Strip lynchets, the remnants of medieval field systems, can be seen in many dales and are particularly obvious in December, when the sun is at a lower angle to the ground (Colin Speakman).

But of daylight. Those short, short precious days, with little more than eight meagre hours of light before darkness starts subtly creeping up on you, are soon gone. This means that to make the most of December you can't afford to waste a moment, planning is of the essence. And it usually means, if you want to get on the hills, getting up early, perhaps before dawn, for an early start.

And it can be deceptive. Two o'clock on a fine December day and you too easily imagine there's a whole long afternoon ahead of you. It is too easy to be tempted out onto a hazardous fell walk, only to be benighted with amazing speed after a couple of hours, darkness and plunging temperatures transforming a seemingly benign hillside into a very formidable place indeed. December days are treacherously brief and must be treated with utmost caution.

But there are two enormous compensations for meagre daylight in an area like the Dales.

The second compensation is the softness of the light. This is something which is difficult, perhaps even impossible to adequately describe in words for it has a very special quality. With the sun always low in the sky, its rays horizontal on the high pastures, everything is sharply defined, lit obliquely. Things you don't normally notice are suddenly in focus, the pattern of stones in a drystone wall, the rich ochre-yellow of lichen on a boulder, the line of long lost ancient field walls or ridges on the hillsides, civilizations long forgotten, their memory there, exposed in winter light. Trees are themselves objects of a new kind of beauty — appearing almost like etchings of themselves, as every twig and branch stands out vividly against the light, as if engraved. Stone bridges, lost beneath scrub and leaves in summer, stand clear and exposed, lit so well by that low angle light that even their masons' marks are clearly decipherable. Detail you simply don't see in the strong light and shade of summer and limestone walls seem to glow in that afternoon light.

In terms of weather the Dales can be totally unpredictable at any time of the year, but in December they are even more so. December might, and so often does, start off by seeming to be a mere extension of autumn although without the glorious colours of October and November, which, by the beginning of the month, have been stripped by a combination of harsh frosts and gales. Temperatures can be deceptively mild, well into the 50s, as if to make you believe that this is a long, late Indian summer with blue skies and the bright red hips in the hedgerows giving a vivid sense of colour contrasted against the brown grey of sandstone walls. Rust-browns of bracken on the hillsides can also give the kind of rich tones that are a photographer's dream. And unlike summer, the temperature is never warm enough to make walking, even uphill, unpleasant and it is not yet cold enough to make sitting or standing a chilly experience.

Yet, those same mild south-westerly airstreams can bring the most ferocious storms which, in a matter of hours, can send trees crashing over narrow roads, turn moorland becks to foaming, impassable rivers and cause sudden flash floods in the valley bottoms that make travel along the ancient lanes a nightmare. Dales rivers can, and do, rise with alarming speed after heavy rain. The Swale is particularly notorious, becoming a raging

The first of these is that for the early part of the month at least, the area is empty of visitors, so that even the most popular haunts enjoy a rare solitude. If you want to discover why eighteenth century travellers 'shivered with horror' at the sight of Gordale Scar, go there on a cold, grey mid-week December morning when nobody is about and soak in the eerie magnificence of those great overhangs. The same place in summer has any such atmosphere totally dissipated by chattering crowds, most of them having strolled up, the couple of hundred yards or so from the lane end out of Malham littering as they go.

In December the Wharfe churns beneath Bolton Bridge but the real spate and floods will follow in the spring after winter's snow (Colin Speakman).

torrent that sweeps walls away, undermines riverside paths, threatens bridges. The Wharfe is almost as ferocious, filling and flooding its banks, a swirling, menacing force, tossing great tree roots and even sizeable boulders like corks.

There's a certain thrill about going up the Dales in the worst weather and being part of the battle between the elements on a heroic scale, trees being wracked by the storm, clouds scudding across escarpments as if to drag them in their path: always assuming, of course, that you're dressed for the part, a waterproof cagoule keeping wind and water at bay. Even a short walk at such times becomes an exciting challenge, even to keep yourself walking upright against a gale whose ferocity intensifies with each foot of height you ascend.

Maybe, by Continental standards, our Dales hills are tiny — at just over 2,000 ft (around 700 metres) they are mere hillocks compared with even the smallest of Alpine ranges. But facing as they do the storms that come straight across the Irish Sea, the first high land from

the Atlantic itself, they take a tremendous physical battering from the weather, making them, in the winter months, as tough as anywhere in the world.

How one appreciates, at such times, the networks of drystone walls that criss-cross the fells, raised by clever builders over many centuries not just to divide upland commons and high pastures, but to provide essential shelter for livestock. Gales and storm-force winds whistle and howl between the stones, but in so doing their force is broken and dissipated, diminishing the power of the wind so that the walls can survive the worst weather. Behind them is shelter for man or beast, and for the walker out in wild weather there is relief, time to catch your breath, enjoy a few moments' respite and maybe a well-earned bite to eat or drink, before renewing the assault.

December can be a very wet month indeed and after several wet days in the Dales, water seems to appear from everywhere. Waterfalls stream down every hillside. Tiny dikes or

Above *The forbidding winter face of Malham Cove* (John C.A. Trotter).

Left *In summer the tourist hordes swamp Malhamdale but at this time of the year the famous limestone pavement above the cove sees only a few, well equipped visitors* (John C.A. Trotter).

Right *When ponds and pools of surface water freeze, walking can be easier in the winter months — but beware a thaw — however temporary!* (Colin Speakman).

Far right *Buckden Gill at the head of Wharfedale is an attractive minor valley at any time, but perhaps never more so than when patches of snow provide a contrasting texture to the rough limestone and scrub vegetation* (Colin Speakman).

streamlets, in normal conditions unnoticed, are major obstacles after a prolonged storm or series of wet days, and streams easily forded in dry weather become murderous torrents requiring careful circumnavigation. Little wonder that many of the old monastic packhorse ways across the heads of the higher Dales had both dry and wet weather routes, the wet weather tracks usually keeping to higher land, using hillsides or ridges, high crossing points with bridges built both for safety and to keep produce dry.

Lower down in the valleys, there are few experiences to beat, for sheer exhilaration, a walk by a Dales river in spate watching the white, foaming breakers on the surface of the river, particularly where they cross hidden obstacles such as buried stepping stones or a flooded milldam. Impressive too is the roar of

the waters, a sound you can sometimes hear half a mile away. Riverside paths often vanish under water, becoming impassable and requiring careful rerouting. But the experience of something truly untamed and barbaric can turn a walk in foul weather into something memorable leaving one with a sense of untamed, brutal power, of pure unleashed energy.

The first winter snows can provide drama of a different kind. It only requires the wind to shift to the north or east for it to pick up the Arctic edge of Greenland, or the Baltic Circle. Temperatures plummet in a matter of hours and, if you're foolish enough to have ignored the forecasts, you're struggling through total blizzard conditions.

But even on less extreme days, I never cease to be amazed at the difference from conditions

in the lower Dales where you start out on a grey, cold day, perhaps with just the odd sleety flake or drift of cold drizzle. Only a few hundred feet up the hillside and you are in a different world, in ice, mist and raging snow conditions. Unless you are prepared with adequate clothing, compass and basic supplies, the consequences can be lethal. If you're out on the tops in a blizzard it can be a frightening experience, however well-equipped. A 'white-out' when moor and sky merge into a featureless haze can whip up out of nowhere and a compass becomes essential to get you safely off a fellside as the temperature drops very quickly indeed. There is only one safe course of action — get off the fells as rapidly as you can.

Snow is less common in the Dales in December than in January, February or March, but rarely a winter goes past without an opening snowstorm, sometimes as early as the end of November, and often in mid or late December, though the sentimental white Christmas is tantalizingly rare. But once the snow has arrived, it can create superb walking conditions. Even the most familiar valley paths can become something rare, new and strange, woods become places of magic, buildings sheer fantasy. Walking through fresh snow can be surprisingly hard work as it drifts behind walls into thigh-deep banks or covers hollows and ditches to bury the unwary to the waist and generally drag your feet back at each and every step. You must allow a lot more time for even the shortest distance after snow has fallen.

Often an anti-cyclone after snow, or even without snow, produces hard frost and superb clear conditions. Sometimes the valleys and

Above *The grandeur of the high ground and its exposure to the elements contrasts with the intimacy of the valleys. In winter one should always be particularly well prepared for a sudden change in the weather* (Colin Speakman).

Right *Even a familiar wall and fence can take on a very different appearance after snow* (Colin Speakman).

Above right *Ribblehead Viaduct is arguably the finest example of railway architecture in the British Isles, but the famous Settle and Carlisle line which runs over it and cost hundreds of lives in the building has suffered the threat of closure in recent years* (Colin Speakman).

towns can lie in fog, whole areas lost in a disgusting freezing murk that hurts the eyes and lungs but, a thousand or more feet above sea level, there usually exists another, brilliantly clear, world. How thrilling it is, on such days, to rise out of the gloom into the crystal sharp light of a perfect day, with the sharpness of light giving views which the warmer, hazier days of summer do not permit.

A further advantage of heavy frost is that soft ground which, in milder conditions is an unpleasant bog (the overused Three Peaks Walk being a classic example) becomes a good firm surface when frozen hard. For the keen fell walker, such conditions offer a marvellous opportunity to explore new and unfamiliar areas. Many areas of the Dales where the going is slow underfoot under normal conditions for all but the most dedicated and foolhardy bogtrotter and perhaps even unsafe, become perfectly passable after frost. Many a great evil moss or bog on a Dales summit is at its best in frosty conditions. Sphagnum peat, wet and boot-trapping in summer, is, after a few days' heavy frost, a firm surface for the walker, a kind of boot-yielding concrete. Places virtually inaccessible in summer are an easy stroll after

frosty weather, so if the weather sets in hard and cold, it is worth taking the opportunity to tackle the less usual peaks and even the places where no formal paths or access is shown.

Travel can be a problem in winter. Driving conditions can be poor, particularly in early mornings when icy roads are a hazard. For the walker wanting to get up into an area like the Dales, buses are limited (Upper Wharfedale is the only valley with anything like a regular bus service) but a superb alternative is to catch a train on the Settle-Carlisle railway which, despite the threat of closure, now has an all-the-year-round Monday to Saturday stopping train service to local stations on the line. This wonderful railway line makes it possible for the walker without a car or reluctant to use his car to leave the thing at home or at a railhead and take the new 'Dalesman' stopping train service, deep into the Dales.

I confess to being a total addict for the Settle-Carlisle line, a railway which doesn't just fringe the edge of the Dales but goes right through the heart of the National Park, opening up something like a third or more of the area to the energetically minded rail user, with Horton-in-Ribblesdale, Ribblehead, Dent,

Garsdale and Kirkby Stephen all being strategically placed for some superb walks. There are also minibus services a couple of days a week to Hawes, Sedbergh and Brough from Garsdale and Kirkby Stephen Stations respectively (you usually have to book your seat in advance — enquire locally) which offer additional possibilities.

This is now truly a line for all seasons. Recent timetable improvements provide a late afternoon return train as well as an early evening train. The service now offers excellent possibilities for short fell walks, for example to the summit of Pen-y-Ghent or Ingleborough, from Horton, from Horton to Ribblehead around Alum Pot, from Dent to Ribblehead via Blea Moor or Whernside, or from Kirkby Stephen to Garsdale along the medieval High Way, a green way which runs along the edge of the fellside from Cotter End to Mallerstang over Hell Gill, the source of the River Eden.

There are few more pleasant experiences on a bright, winter's morning than to catch the train from Leeds or Skipton for example, along this most magnificent of railway lines, superbly engineered over its entire length, but most magnificent of all as it emerges from Blea Moor Tunnel to contour around the head of Dentdale, some 1,100 ft above sea level, and then to alight, maybe at Dent Station, and, as the train trundles out of the platform behind you, to sense the quietness and beauty all around. It's something you don't get when you arrive by car, which keeps its intrusive suburban presence attached to you as if by a giant, invisible umbilical cord which forces you to return to your parked vehicle, the inevitable circular walk dictated by it. But come by train, and once the train has gone so has urban civilization — the Dales are yours. It's a new kind of freedom — freedom from the ubiquity of the automobile.

Not only are there stations to start a walk from but stations to end a walk at, in most cases with handily situated cafes or pubs close to them, a facility particularly welcome in late autumn or winter. Finish a walk at Garsdale, for example: there's no need to hang about on the cold station platform longer than you need to, with the Moorcock Inn less than a mile away. Then there's the Station Inn at the bottom of the Station Drive to Ribblehead Station whilst Horton gives the choice of the Crown Inn or the excellent Pen-y-Ghent Café in the village centre, specialising in hungry

ramblers' needs. If you are out late into a December afternoon, perhaps coming off the fells as daylight begins to drain away in the west and lights start to appear in the scattered farms along the valley, faint beacons of civilization as the cold bites through your gloves, you can be assured that in these places your share of warmth and seasonal comfort lies ahead.

And what could be more satisfying than to see the bright headlights and long line of the carriage windows of a train through the darkness as it comes around the curve over a viaduct towards you, to scoop you up again out of the threatening blackness of a Dales night and take you back to your everyday world and creature comforts? Nor does it

matter if, after a day in the cold, you find yourself nodding off to sleep on the train, although that is a real danger for the fell walker having to motor any distance.

Such are the pleasures of December walking by train. Romantic perhaps. But trains are about romance, and so are the Dales themselves and the combination of the two is intoxicating. Forget nostalgia, concentrate on the quality of the experience today and enjoy both the trains and the fell country, for they offer something very special indeed for anyone who loves this landscape.

December has another major compensation — Christmas. For most people Christmas is the first break from the routine of office or factory since the summer vacations, the longest period of the year without any statutory holiday. And no longer is the break confined to the formal holidays — Christmas Day, Boxing Day and New Year. In many cases shops and factories are closed for the intervening period, in some cases a full ten days if the intervening weekends are included.

A winter break in the Dales is an attractive proposition, particularly as the area has an

Grassington Bridge is typical of the stone packhorse bridges of varying sizes to be found in almost every dale (Colin Speakman).

excellent choice of accommodation from small country hotels and traditional inns, to guest houses, farmhouses, Youth Hostels and that relatively recent development, the Bunkhouse Barn — former barns on Dales farms converted to simple self-catering accommodation, though with facilities, including showers, kitchens and drying rooms that are far from Spartan. There are also self-catering cottages to be had and these are always popular over the Christmas period. The attractions of spending Christmas in the Dales are self-evident. The peace, the beauty, the opportunity to get out into the countryside from your front door are precious things for the town dweller. There's also the intrinsic charm of the Dales villages themselves, and that remarkable institution, the Dales pub, though at that time of the year most occupants are likely to be 'off-come'd uns' and locals have a hard time to get to the bar.

I am fortunate enough to live on the edge of the Dales, which means that only a short drive or walk takes me into the heartland of the National Park, and the Christmas break is invariably a marvellous opportunity to renew acquaintance with favourite paths. Christmas tends to be the season of over-indulgence. Too much food and too much alcohol induce a kind of apathetic mental and physical torpor. The best remedy for this, apart, of course, from a strict mineral water diet, is a vigorous walk through or across a Yorkshire Dale, an experience which will improve the circulation of the blood and get honest Yorkshire air into the lungs, in a manner calculated to please anyone's cardiologist.

But often Christmas is a family occasion with older people and children around, when a hard day on the tops, as enchanting as it would be in some respects, can be considered anti-social. The need, whether you're staying in the area or simply visiting for a day, is often for the kind of short walk with a focal point, perhaps a fine viewpoint, which can be undertaken in a short day or an afternoon during the holiday period. We have a number of favourites for just such an occasion. There's Fountains Abbey, for example, not just the celebrated Cistercian ruins and eighteenth century water gardens, but the superb deerpark. A circular walk which takes in both offers a heritage and landscape afternoon ideal for December.

Not far away, at Brimham Rocks, in Nidderdale, another National Trust property open in December offers the possibility of a short winter afternoon's walk around the wind-carved gritstone crags, each with a fanciful Victorian name and superb views over into Nidderdale and across the Vale of York to the Moors and York Minster itself. Then there's Beamsley Beacon, near Addingham, Wharfedale, one of the great chain of beacons which crossed Northern England in Tudor times and which was used to warn the region of the advance of the Spanish Armada in 1588. You can walk there from Ilkley or Addingham, or even from the road below the Beacon itself, and the view from the summit across the Dale given clear weather is quite superb.

Ilkley Moor, with or without the legendary hat, is another place where even a couple of hours walking can rid the head and lungs of Yuletide stuffiness: the views from the moorland ridge above Cow and Calf Rocks, or over at the Bronze Age Swastika Stone across central Wharfedale are quite magnificent, whilst an old favourite of West Yorkshire ramblers is to cross the moor by paved path to Dick Hudson's pub above Bingley, in Airedale — a splendid winter walk, though perhaps best done in the opposite direction, from Bingley to Ilkley.

Christmas Day itself is the kind of occasion where a short, special, beautiful walk has to be fitted in between other family events, a badly needed bit of fresh air. For us, Bolton Abbey is high on the list — the magically beautiful setting of the priory itself can be enjoyed over a couple of hours' stroll through the adjacent woods by the River Wharfe, a landscape immortalized by Turner, Landseer and Ruskin, or you can extend your stroll for a full afternoon's walk through the gloriously beautiful Strid Woods, the rocks of the wood covered with intense green mosses, and take in the spectacle of the Strid itself — a narrow gorge, barely a yard wide where many have leapt to their death — as impressive in its awesome beauty in December as at any time of the year, but beware the river in spate. And if you decide to spend the whole day out of doors, then there's a temptation if the weather's fine, to take in one of the loveliest of

---

Set on a meander of the River Wharfe, the ruins of Bolton Abbey, picked out against a late December sky, seem perfectly in harmony with their surroundings (Simon Warner).

all Dales hilltops, Simon Seat, easily reached from the Cavendish Pavilion area below Bolton Abbey Woods through the Valley of Desolation and the moorland path through the National Park Access Area, returning via Howgill and The Strid. Don't expect to do this and be back for Christmas lunch, but for a Boxing Day walk, for example, and burning off a few excess calories, it'll take some beating.

Water, whether frozen or liquid, always provides a good focal point for winter walking. The Dales aren't normally known for their lakes, with the notable exception of Malham Tarn and Semerwater. But in fact, the eastern Dales are dominated by a series of man-made lakes that has led them to be described as 'Yorkshire's Lake District' This area includes Washburndale and Nidderdale.

The Washburn Valley, a tributary of the Wharfe, north of Otley, is little known outside Leeds or Bradford, but in fact contains a superb area of countryside, and a chain of four reservoirs, Thrushcross, Fewston, Swinsty and Lindley Wood, all of which offer delightful winter walking, rich in birdlife as waterfowl use the lakes as sanctuaries. Paths around the water edge make it simple to plan pleasant circular strolls, never more enjoyable than on fine winter afternoons when afternoon light quickly becomes tinged with orange and pink as the sun begins to set.

Higher up the dales, Upper Nidderdale's two dalehead reservoirs of Scar House and Angram are again ideal places for short winter rambles. A Water Authority toll road allows cars to drive right up from Lofthouse to Scar House Reservoir. A walk across the great reservoir dam and around the reservoir itself gives a feeling of being in the centre of wild fell country, never more so than when a high wind whips the waves of the reservoir into great breakers, lashing over the dam like a storm-tossed sea.

The Dales are particularly rich in waterfalls but if there's been a heavy rainfall, the floodwaters make a mighty cataract from a slender trickle. On the other hand, if it's been dry and frosty over a period, frozen spray and icicles transform a fall into something amazingly beautiful. There's such a tremendous choice of falls in the Dales that it is difficult to choose any at random, but there are three which are not only beautiful in their own right, but can all be incorporated in a short stroll. The first is Mill Gill Force in Wensleydale, easily reached from Askrigg along a well signed woodland path; the second is Hardraw Force, England's highest single drop fall, reached by fieldpath (the Pennine Way) from Hawes, or at Hardraw itself, by going through the Green Dragon Inn (small toll payable). And perhaps the loveliest of all,

Catrigg Force, in Ribblesdale, a short but extremely steep walk from Stainforth following steps into a hidden gorge where the fall plunges down a narrow chasm.

If it's waterfalls you're after, another idea for a winter walk when the weather's not too good is the 4½-mile Ingleton waterfalls walk. The advantage here, of course, is that as the falls are in a series of deep glens along the Rivers Greta and Doe you are out of the worst of the wind and the rain, whilst a good head of water roaring down the falls increases their spectacle. These are entirely artificial walkways, hence the entrance fee, with steps, handrails and bridges to give a better view of the series of cataracts and falls; nonetheless, the paths can be dangerous in wet conditions and care is needed. Thornton Force at the summit of the gorge is particularly impressive with a narrow ledge along which, if you are careful, you can walk, to stand behind that glittering wall of water — a feat not to be attempted, however, when the stream is in flood.

One of my particular December favourites is Clapdale, easily reached from Clapham, that

Far left *Rylston Cross, Wharfedale, stands tall in all weathers — a minor monument, perhaps, but one, no doubt, of great meaning to those who raised it* (Colin Speakman).

Left *The delightful Janet's Foss in Malhamdale* (Colin Speakman).

loveliest of Dales villages. Clapham has the advantage for public transport users of being on both a bus route (Pennine Motors from Skipton) and rail line (the Leeds-Skipton-Lancaster line) though Clapham Station is 1½ miles from the village. From the National Park visitor centre in Clapham it's a short walk through the village, on either side of the stream, to the entrance to the Ingleborough Estate through the woodyard (admission charge payable) and along the estate path which now forms part of the Reginald Farrer Trail. Many of the ornamental trees along the route were planted by this world famous botanist and plant collector in the early years of this century before his tragically early death in the mountains of Burma. The track follows the edge of the lake to Ingleborough Cave and Trow Gill, an extraordinary dry limestone valley from where a return to Clapham can be made along Clapdale Lane, the footpath running parallel and above the estate track. Alternatively, continue along the Farrer Trail to return via Long Lane and Thwaite Lane, under the curious tunnels which go beneath the Ingleborough Hall gardens back into the village.

Clapdale provides, of course, an excellent route to the summit of Ingleborough mountain itself via the extraordinary mouth of Gaping Gill, a pothole large enough to contain the whole of St Paul's Cathedral. And when the year comes to an end, there is something positively satisfying about climbing a major Dales peak, perhaps Ingleborough itself, or Pen-y-Ghent or maybe over to the east, those almost equally impressive summits of Buckden Pike, Great Whernside or Pen Hill. Perhaps it's because a hill top gives you a sense of perspective, allowing you to look down on mere humanity and its trivial affairs down below you. The end of a year is a time to look back, to take stock, to plan ahead. Maybe *that* is why climbing a mountain on the last day of December — Old Year's Day — is such a satisfying experience, a kind of rounding off of all that's gone before.

I remember one such Old Year's Day just a few years ago. There had been snow on Boxing Day and the weather remained freezing cold, with severe frosts each night, but giving dry, still, sunny days. I have never seen the Dales more magical than they were on that occasion, the hills covered in snow and brilliantly lit, each ridge clearly defined and seemingly greater, grander, wilder than in summer, a sub-Alpine landscape of stunning beauty.

We climbed Pen-y-Ghent, the mountain set against the deep, deep blueness of the sky as impressive as any Alpine peak. On the wire sheep fences above the walls on the final summit ridge snow was carved into delicate, fantastic shapes, blown by the wind and frozen hard. The summit views were unbelievable, as if the Alps or the Arctic had stretched out a great arm to reconquer Ingleborough, the great curve of Fountains Fell, Foxup Moor and the top of Littondale like a new Ice Age dawning.

Here indeed is my 'bit of landscape'. What could summer ever do to compare with such splendours?

Colin Speakman is a well known writer on the Yorkshire Dales. His publications include *Walking in the Yorkshire Dales, A Portrait of North Yorkshire* and *The Dales Way*. He is the Northern Correspondent of *The Great Outdoors*. He lives on the edge of Ilkley Moor, Wharfedale, and is part-time Secretary of the Yorkshire Dales Society, editing the Society's quarterly journal *The Yorkshire Dales Review*.